Maths Matters Plus Book

Joyce Chester ■ Eon Harper ■ Gerry Price

CONTENTS

The Ice Bowl 2	Growing up 50
When shall I marry? 4	Electric Charge 52
Why Wait? 6	Blocks and Cubes 54
Posting for Christmas 8	Crime News 56
Party Punch 10	Rotating Patterns 58
In the Charts 12	Going Home 60
Ski Trip 14	Mind that Child! 62
Angles and Turning 16	Parcel Post 64
Pot Black 18	Fuel Savers 66
If he stops, can you? 20	Sequences 68
Work Experience 22	U-Boat Attack 70
Shapes on Screen 24	On the road 72
Paper Folds 26	Folding Triangles 74
Lanbourne Pottery 28	Check it out 76
Sun Seeking 30	Display stands 78
What's it worth? 32	Dominoes 80
Return Ticket 34	The Nielson Line 82
Pop Prints 36	Decision Trees 84
Using Maths 38	Designing a House 86
Dream Kitchen 40	Oil at Sea 88
Aircrash 42	Instant Credit 90
Phone Charges 44	A Place to Live 92
Hill Climb 46	Finding a name 94
Connections 48	Working with eight 96

Longman

Longman Group UK Limited
Longman House, Burnt Mill, Harlow, Essex CM20 2JE, England and Associated Companies throughout the World.

© Addison-Wesley Publishers Limited 1980
This edition © Longman Group UK Limited 1990
First published by Addison-Wesley Publishers Limited 1980
This edition first published by Longman Group UK Limited 1991
Second impression 1992
Set in 11/13 Helvetica
Printed in Hong Kong
CALAY/02

All rights reserved. No part of this publication may be reproduced, stored in a retrieval system, or transmitted in any form or by any means, electronic, mechanical, photocopying, recording or otherwise, without either the prior written permission of the Publishers or a licence permitting restricted copying in the United Kingdom issued by the Copyright Licensing Agency Ltd, 90 Tottenham Court Road, London, W1P 9HE.

ISBN 0 582 22528 0

The Ice Bowl

A new ice skating rink has just opened in Tadley.

1. How many FREE 'N' EASY sessions are there each week?

2. How many sessions are there specially for under 16s each week?

3. What is the charge per person for:
   a. a weekday GENERAL session?
   b. the Friday night DISCO session?
   c. the Thursday night FREE 'N' EASY session?

4. What would it cost for four people to go to the Wednesday night DISCO session, including skate hire?

THE ICE BOWL

JUST LOOK AT THE PRICES!!

GENERAL   per person
Monday – Friday   10.00 am – 4.00 pm   £1.10
Saturday   2.30 pm – 5.00 pm   £1.25
Sunday   12.30 pm – 4.00 pm   £1.50

JUNIOR DISCO (16 years and under)
Tuesday   5.00 pm – 6.30 pm   £1.00
Friday, Saturday   5.30 pm – 7.30 pm   £1.25

FREE 'N' EASY
Tuesday, Thursday   8.00 pm – 11.00 pm   £1.50
Sunday   10.00 pm – 12.30 pm   £1.50

DISCO
Monday, Wednesday, Sunday   8.00 pm – 11.00 pm   £1.50
Friday, Saturday   8.00 pm – 11.00 pm   £1.85

CHILDREN'S FUN TIME (16 years and under)
Saturday   10.00 am – 12.30 pm   £1.00

Skate hire 70p per session

The Cashier at the Ice Bowl uses a ready reckoner to work out the cost of tickets.

5. Copy this ready reckoner. Fill it in.

6. Use your ready reckoner to work out the cost for:
   a. 3 people at Saturday's JUNIOR DISCO.
   b. 5 people at Sunday's GENERAL session, including skate hire.
   c. 4 people at Saturday's DISCO, two with skate hire and two using their own skates.

No. of Tickets \ Price	£1.10	£1.25	£1.50	£1.85	£0.70
1	£1.10				
2	£2.20				
3					
4				£6.00	£2.80
5					
6					

7. What change from £10 will the cashier give if you pay for six people for the Saturday GENERAL session, and skate hire for two?

The Ice Bowl

The Ice Bowl opened on Friday 12th April.

These are the attendance figures for the opening day.

Day		Session		
		GENERAL	JUNIOR DISCO	DISCO
Friday	skaters	46	64	190
	skate hire	12	40	136

8 a Which of the three sessions was most popular?
   b How many attended this session?

9 a On Friday how many skaters were there altogether?
   b How many hired skates?

10 Work out the total takings for Friday. You will need to look at the Ice Bowl price list on the opposite page.

These are the attendance figures for the first 3 days the Ice Bowl was open.

Day		Session				
		CHILDREN'S FUN TIME	GENERAL	JUNIOR DISCO	DISCO	FREE 'N' EASY
Friday	Skaters		46	64	190	
	Skate hire		12	40	136	
Saturday	Skaters	59	89	134	265	
	Skate hire	45	68	108	183	
Sunday	Skaters		92		124	62
	Sakte hire		64		98	40

11 Which session during the first 3 days attracted most skaters?

12 Which of the three days was the busiest?

13 Work out how much money was taken each day.

14 What were the total receipts for the three days?

When shall I marry?

One hundred 16-year olds were asked the question:

When do you want to get married?

Key
stands for 2 girls
stands for 2 boys

This is what they said.

1 Look at the key. What does:
   a stand for?
   b stand for?

'When I'm 17.'	
'When I'm 18.'	
'When I'm 19.'	
'When I'm 20.'	
'When I'm 21.'	
'When I'm 22.'	
'When I'm 23.'	
'When I'm 24.'	
'When I'm 25.'	
'When I'm 28.'	
'When I'm 30.'	
'Never.'	

2 How many girls said:
   a 'When I'm 17.'
   b 'When I'm 25.'
   c 'When I'm 21.'?

3 Copy this table. Fill it in.

4 a How many girls altogether answered the question?
   b How many boys answered it?

Age		17	18	19	20	21	22	23	24	25	28	30	Never
Number who want to get married	Girls	2	5	6									
	Boys	0	0										
	Total	2											

When shall I marry?

5 Copy this bar chart and finish it.

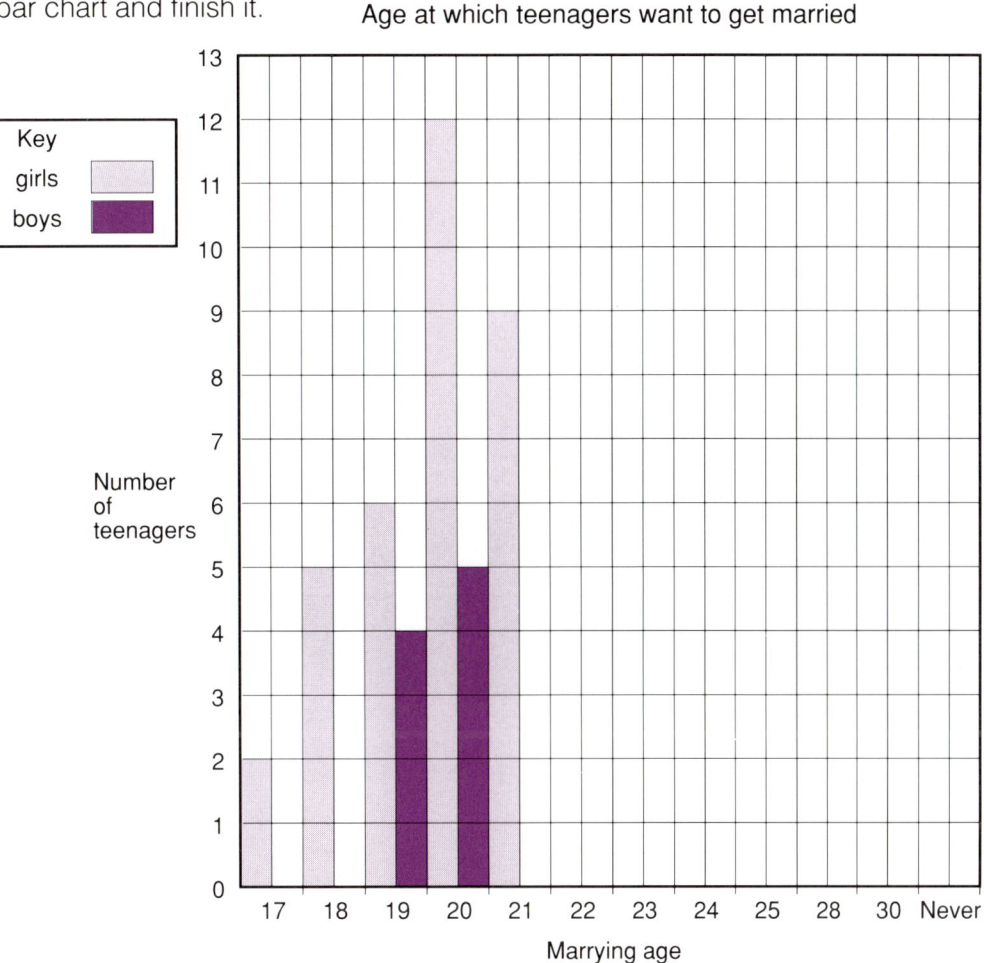

Age at which teenagers want to get married

Key
girls ▫
boys ▪

(Number of teenagers vs Marrying age: 17, 18, 19, 20, 21, 22, 23, 24, 25, 28, 30, Never)

6 What was the most popular age chosen to get married:
   a by girls?
   b by boys?

7 How many girls wanted to get married:
   a before they were 20?
   b when they were 25 or over?

8 How many boys wanted to get married:
   a before they were 20?
   b when they were 25 or over?

More boys than girls said they wanted to get married when they were 23.

9 Write down the other ages chosen by more boys than girls.

10 Do you think it is generally true that girls want to get married younger than boys? Explain your answer.

5

Why Wait?

John wants to buy this radio cassette player on hire-purchase (h.p.).

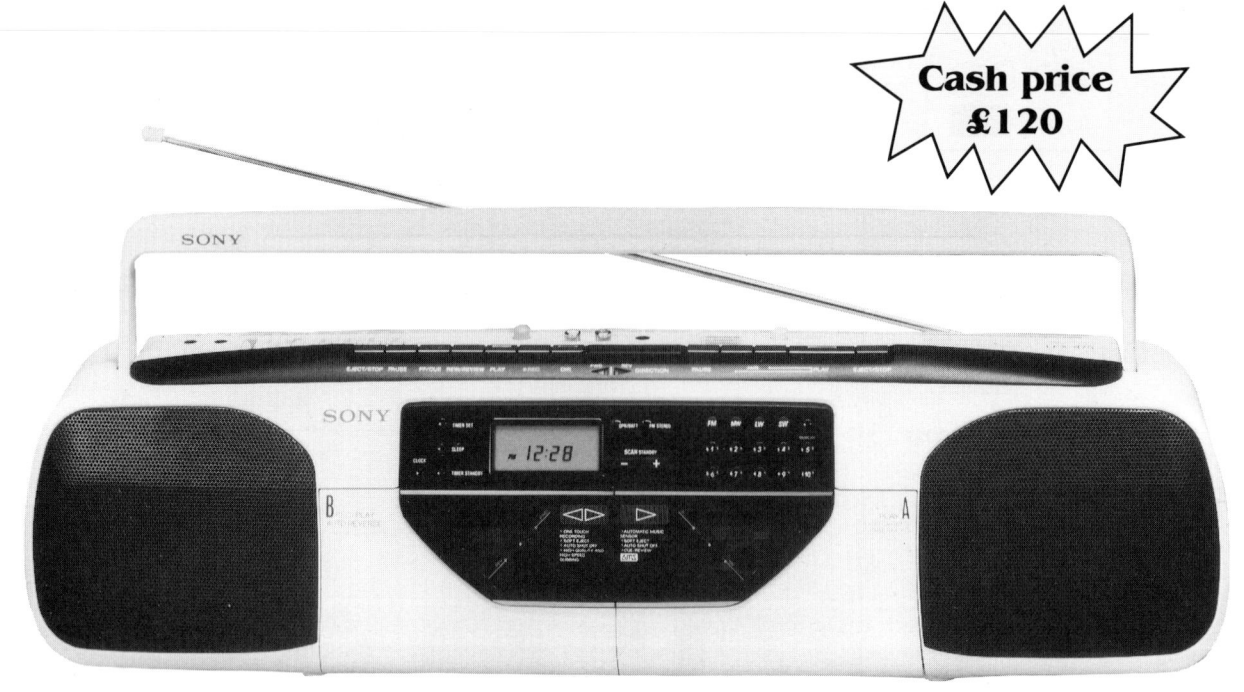

Cash price £120

Buy Now!

Available on hire-purchase
★ 20% deposit
★ balance can be paid over:
    9 months
   12 months
   18 months
   24 months

1 What is its cash price?

2 What is the longest time John can take to pay for it on h.p.?

John has to pay a 20% cash deposit before he can take it away.

3 What is:
   a 10% of £120?
   b 20% of £120?

4 What cash deposit must John pay?

5 What balance will he have to pay off?

John pays off the balance monthly.

The shopkeeper uses this chart to work out the monthly repayments.

Balance left to pay	Monthly repayments over:			
	9 months	12 months	18 months	24 months
£94	£11.82	£9.20	£6.58	£5.43
£95	£11.95	£9.30	£6.66	£5.48
£96	£12.07	£9.39	£6.73	£5.53
£97	£12.20	£9.49	£6.80	£5.58
£98	£12.32	£9.59	£6.86	£5.63
£99	£12.45	£9.69	£6.94	£5.69

6 What are the monthly repayments on John's balance over:
   a 9 months?
   b 12 months?
   c 18 months?
   d 24 months?

John can afford to pay up to £10 a month.

7 What is the **least** number of months he can afford to spread his payments over?

8 On this repayment scheme how much would he repay:
   a each month?
   b in 12 months?

9 a How much would he pay altogether for the radio cassette?
   b How much more than the cash price is this?

MAKING A CHOICE

10 Copy this table. Fill it in.

Balance	Number of monthly payments	Monthly repayment	Total repayment	Deposit	Total h.p. price
£96	9			£24	
£96	12		£112.68	£24	£136.68
£96	18			£24	
£96	24			£24	

11 How much more than the cash price would the radio cassette cost if John paid over:
   a 9 months?
   b 12 months?
   c 18 months?
   d 24 months?

12 Which repayment scheme would you choose? Why?

Posting for Christmas

Maureen's boyfriend Winston works in Germany. Her grandparents live in Jamaica.

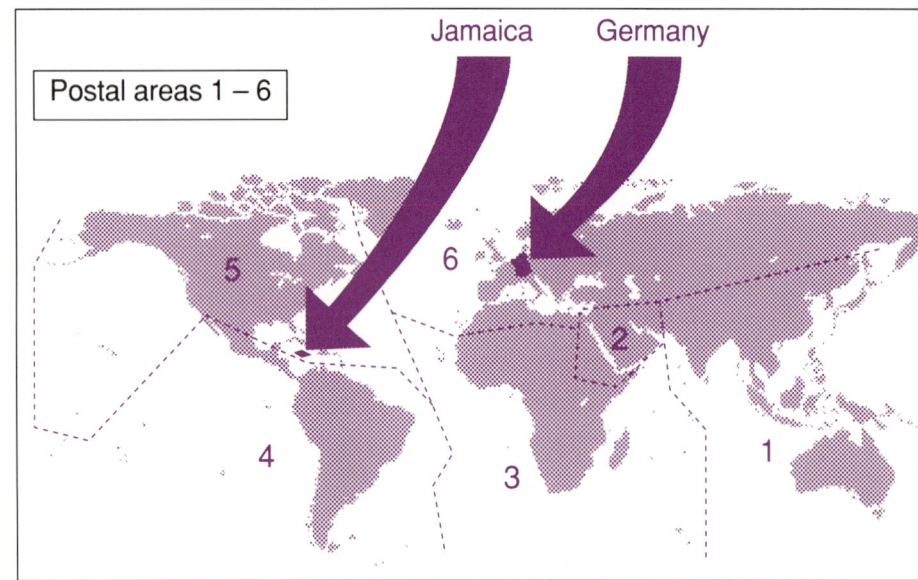

Postal areas 1 – 6

She is sending them presents and cards for Christmas.

Destination	Area	Parcels and Packets Surface	Parcels and Packets Air	Christmas cards and Printed Papers Surface	Letters and Postcards Air
Far East and Australia	1	9 Oct	4 Dec	11 Oct	6 Dec
Middle and Near East	2	16 Oct	4 Dec	18 Oct	11 Dec
Africa (except North)	3	16 Oct	4 Dec	18 Oct	6 Dec
Central and South America	4	1 Nov	4 Dec	3 Nov	6 Dec
Canada, U.S.A. and West Indies	5	1 Nov	4 Dec	6 Nov	4 Dec
Europe and North Africa	6	27 Nov	6 Dec	27 Nov	11 Dec

Last posting dates for Christmas

Posting to Jamaica.

1 What is the last date Maureen should post a Christmas card to her grandparents?
2 What is the last date she should post them a parcel:
    a by surface mail?
    b by airmail?

Posting for Christmas

This is the page for November from Maureen's calendar.

3. Maureen posted her grandparents' card on 4th November.
   What day of the week was this?

4. She posted their parcel by airmail on the last Wednesday of November.
   What date was this?

5. What day of the week is:
   a 30th November?
   b 1st December?

6. Copy this page for December. Fill it in.

7. Maureen's grandparents' card arrived on 16th December.
   a What day of the week was this?
   b How many days did it take to arrive?

8. Their parcel arrived 18 days after Maureen posted it. What date did it arrive?

November						
Sun	Mon	Tues	Wed	Thur	Fri	Sat
				1	2	3
4	5	6	7	8	9	10
11	12	13	14	15	16	17
18	19	20	21	22	23	24
25	26	27	28	29	30	

December						
Sun	Mon	Tues	Wed	Thur	Fri	Sat

Posting to Germany.

9. Maureen sent Winston's present by surface mail on the last possible posting date.
   a What date was this?
   b What day of the week was this?

10. She sent him an airmail letter exactly 2 weeks later. What date was this?

11. Do you think the letter arrived in time for Christmas? Why?

Party Punch

The Youth Club is planning a barbecue.

These are the recipes for the drinks the club wants to make.

Southern Delight
Makes 20 glasses:

1 litre cider
250 millilitres white wine
800 millilitres orange juice
600 millilitres tonic water
150 millilitres grapefruit juice

Florida Punch
Makes 20 glasses:

1 litre cider
250 millilitres white wine
700 millilitres orange juice
500 millilitres tonic water
250 millilitres lime juice
100 millilitres grapefruit juice

1 a How many litres of cider are needed for each recipe?
  b How much cider is needed altogether?

2 How many millilitres of white wine are needed for 20 glasses of:
  a Southern Delight?
  b Florida Punch?

3 How much white wine is needed if 20 glasses of each drink are made?
  Give your answer: a in millilitres
                      b in litres.

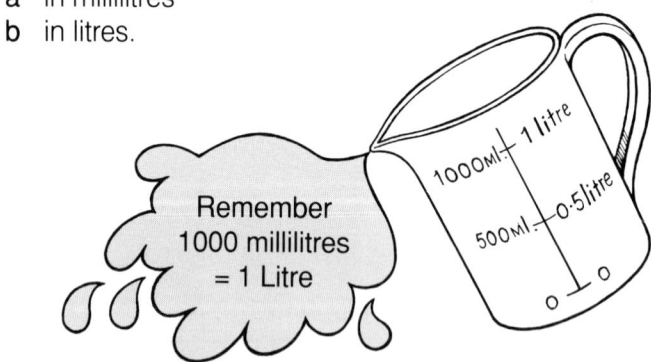

Remember
1000 millilitres
= 1 Litre

The Youth Club decides to make enough for 80 glasses of each recipe.

4 How many litres of cider will be needed:
  a for each recipe?
  b altogether?

5 How many millilitres of wine will be needed:
  a for each recipe?
  b altogether?

6 How many litres of wine will be needed altogether?

Party Punch

7 Copy this table and fill it in.

	Amount needed to make 80 glasses		Total	
	Southern Delight	Florida Punch	millilitres	litres
Cider	4ℓ	4ℓ	8000	8
White Wine	1000 mℓ	1000 mℓ	2000	2
Orange Juice	3200 mℓ			
Tonic Water				
Grapefruit Juice				
Lime Juice				

The ingredients for the drinks are sold like this.

white wine 700 mℓ

tonic water 500 mℓ

cider 1ℓ

lime juice 1ℓ

orange juice 1ℓ
grapefruit juice 1ℓ

8 a How many millilitres are there in a bottle of tonic water?
   b How many bottles of tonic water make up 1 litre?

9 How many bottles of tonic water will the Youth Club need to buy?

SHOPPING LIST

10 Make a list of all the ingredients the Youth Club will need for the drinks.
Write down by the side of each how many bottles or cartons should be bought.

In the Charts

You work in Clark's record shop. It is your job to order records.

City Nights, *You Walk By* and *Rock Beat* are the latest singles from 3 top groups.
This is the sales graph for the first 4 weeks.

1. How many copies of *City Nights* were sold:
   a. in the first week?
   b. in the first 2 weeks?
   c. in the first 4 weeks?

2. In the first 4 weeks how many copies were sold:
   a. of *You Walk By*?
   b. of *Rock Beat*?

3. Two of the records went into the charts.
   Which do you think they were?

4. Sales of one record were still climbing after 4 weeks.
   Which record was it?

You order records every 4 weeks.
You started with 150 copies of each record.

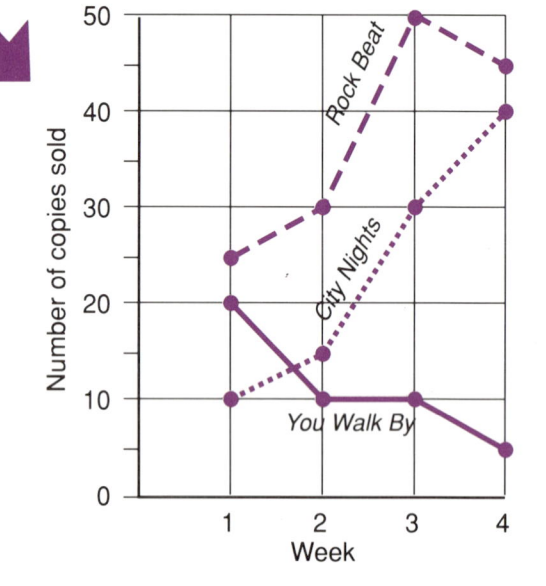

5. Copy this table. Fill in the second and third columns.

Record	First 4 weeks order	Number sold	Number left in stock	Second 4 weeks order	Number in stock
City Nights	150	95	55		
You walk by	150				
Rock Beat	150				

In the Charts

You have to decide how many records to order for the second 4 weeks.

Look at the sales graph.

6 How many copies of *City Nights* do you think will be sold:
  a in week 5?
  b in the second 4 weeks?

7 How many copies of *City Nights* do you think should be ordered for the second 4 weeks? (Remember there are 55 left in stock.) Write your answer in your table.

8 How many copies do you think will be sold in the second 4 weeks of:
  a *You Walk By*?
  b *Rock Beat*?

9 How many copies of each record do you think should be ordered for the second 4 weeks? Write your answers in your table.

10 Fill in the last column of your table.

These were the sales at Clark's for the second 4 weeks.

Record	Number of copies sold each week			
	Week 5	Week 6	Week 7	Week 8
City Nights	45	50	40	30
You Walk By	5	3	0	0
Rock Beat	40	30	25	25

11 Work out how many copies of each record were sold in the second 4 weeks.

12 Look at the number of copies sold and the number you ordered. Did you have enough of each record in stock?

NEW ORDER

13 Make a copy of the graph opposite on centimetre squared paper. Extend it to show the sales for all 8 weeks.

14 Use the graph to help you to decide how many of each record will be sold in weeks 9 to 12.

15 How many of each record will you need to order?

Ski Trip

Jennifer is going skiing in Austria with her school. The map shows the route her coach will take.

1. Through which countries does the coach pass on the way to Austria?

2. In which countries does the coach stop for meals?

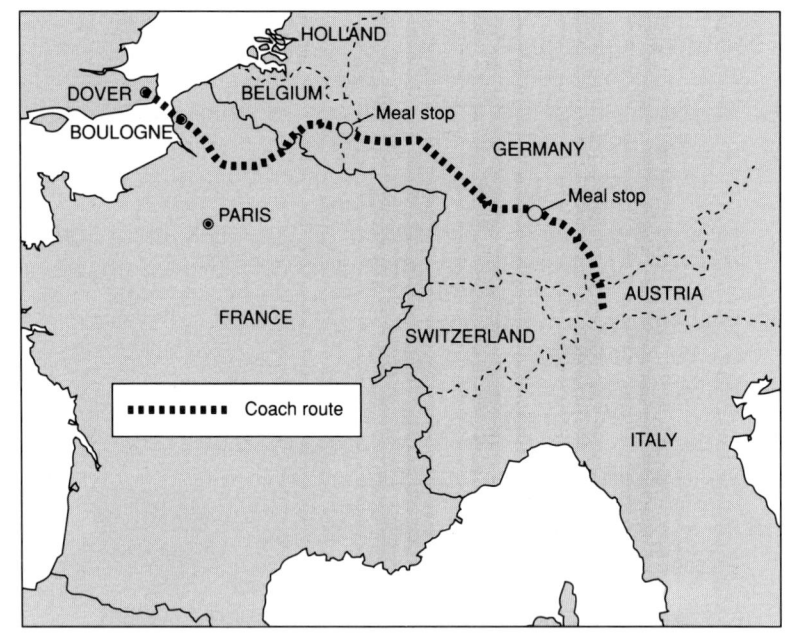

In Belgium 1 franc is worth about 1½p.

3. Copy this exchange rate table. Fill it in.

Belgian Francs	10	20	30	40	50	100	200
Sterling (£p)							

4. Here are some of the items Jennifer can buy at the motorway services in Belgium. Work out the cost of each in sterling (£p).

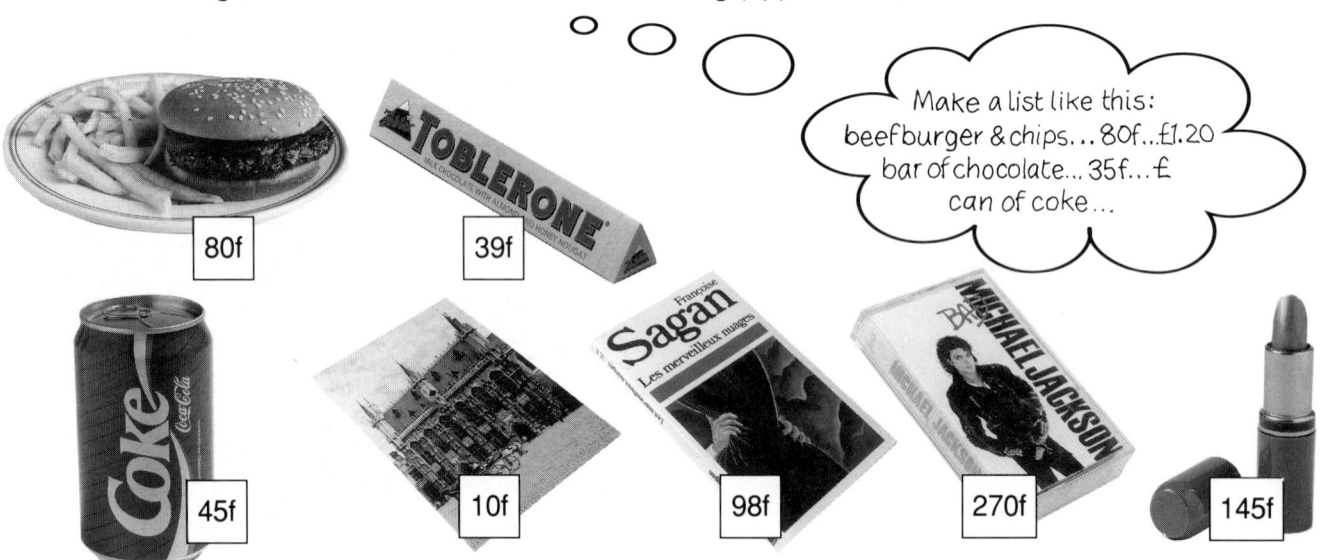

Make a list like this:
beefburger & chips... 80f... £1.20
bar of chocolate... 35f... £
can of coke...

- beefburger & chips 80f
- Toblerone 39f
- can of Coke 45f
- postcard 10f
- Sagan book 98f
- Michael Jackson cassette 270f
- lipstick 145f

5. On the outward journey Jennifer buys a can of coke and a lipstick in Belgium. How much do these cost altogether:
   a. in Belgian money?
   b. in English money?

Ski Trip

In Germany 10 pfennigs are worth about 3 pence.

6 Copy this exchange rate table. Fill it in.

pfennigs (pf)	10	20	30	40	50	100	200	500	1000
sterling (£p)									

7 In Germany 100 pfennigs make 1 Deutschemark (Dm).
   a About how much in Sterling is 1 Deutschemark?
   b About how many Deutschemark are there to £1?

8 Look at the price list for the German motorway services. Work out the cost of each item in sterling (£p).

9 Jennifer buys beefburger and chips, apfeltorte and cola at the Autobahn Service:
   What is their total cost:
   a in German money,
   b in English money?

10 Which items on the list are more expensive in Germany than in Belgium?

AUTOBAHN SERVICE

Beefburger & chips ....6.50 Dm
Kirschtorte ....4.50 Dm
Apfeltorte ....4.25 Dm
Holsten pils ....3.20 Dm
Cola ....2.50 Dm
Chocolate ....1.95 Dm
Books ....10.75 Dm
Postcards ....50 pf
Lipstick ....7.50 Dm

AUSTRIAN MONEY

The school only allows Jennifer to take £50 pocket money altogether.
She will be staying in Austria for six days.

11 How much of each foreign currency do you think Jennifer should take with her. Remember to allow some money for meals each way.
   (£1 = 22 Austrian Schillings).

Angles and Turning

The pointer is turning in a clockwise direction.
From diagram A to diagram L it makes a **full turn (a whole turn)**.

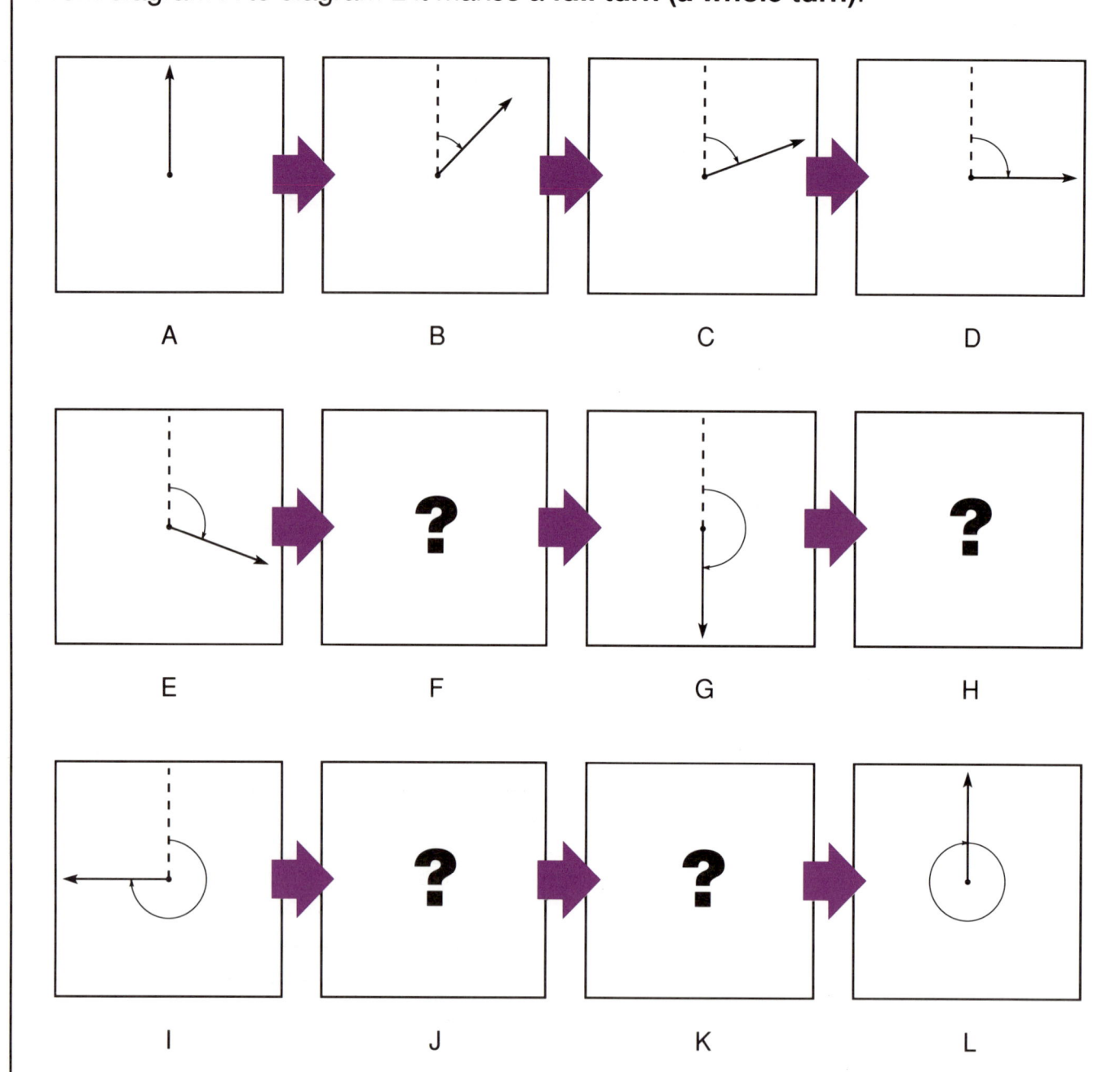

A   B   C   D

E   F   G   H

I   J   K   L

1   Which diagram shows the pointer when it has made:
    a a $\frac{1}{4}$ turn,   **b** a $\frac{1}{2}$ turn,   **c** a $\frac{3}{4}$ turn?

2   Sketch your own possible diagrams for F, H, J and K.

3   Diagram D shows the pointer when it has made a $\frac{1}{4}$ turn. Angles less than a $\frac{1}{4}$ turn are called **acute** angles. Which diagrams show the pointer when it has turned through an acute angle?

16

Angles and Turning

4 A $\frac{1}{4}$ turn is called a **right angle**.
   How many right angles has the pointer turned
   through in: **a** D,   **b** G,   **c** I,   **d** L?

5 Angles which are larger than 1 right angle but smaller
   than 2 right angles are called **obtuse** angles. Which
   diagrams show obtuse angles?

6 Angles which are larger than 2 right angles are called **reflex**
   angles. Diagram I shows a reflex angle. Which other diagrams show
   a reflex angle?

7 In this figure the types of angle inside it are marked.
   Copy the letter T.
   Mark and label each angle 'acute', 'right', 'obtuse' or 'reflex'.

TRIANGLE AND QUADRILATERAL CHALLENGE

8 **a** This triangle has one right angle and two acute angles.
        Draw a triangle which has three acute angles.
   b What other possibilities are there for the types of angles a
        triangle can have?
        List them like this: right, acute, acute
                              acute, acute, acute
                               ...   .
                               ...   .
                               ...   .
        Make a drawing for each example
   c What possibilities are there for the types of angle a quadrilateral (four-sided figure) can have?
        List them like this: right,   right,   right,   right.
                               ...   .
                               ...   .
                               ...   .
                               ...   .
        Make a drawing for each example.

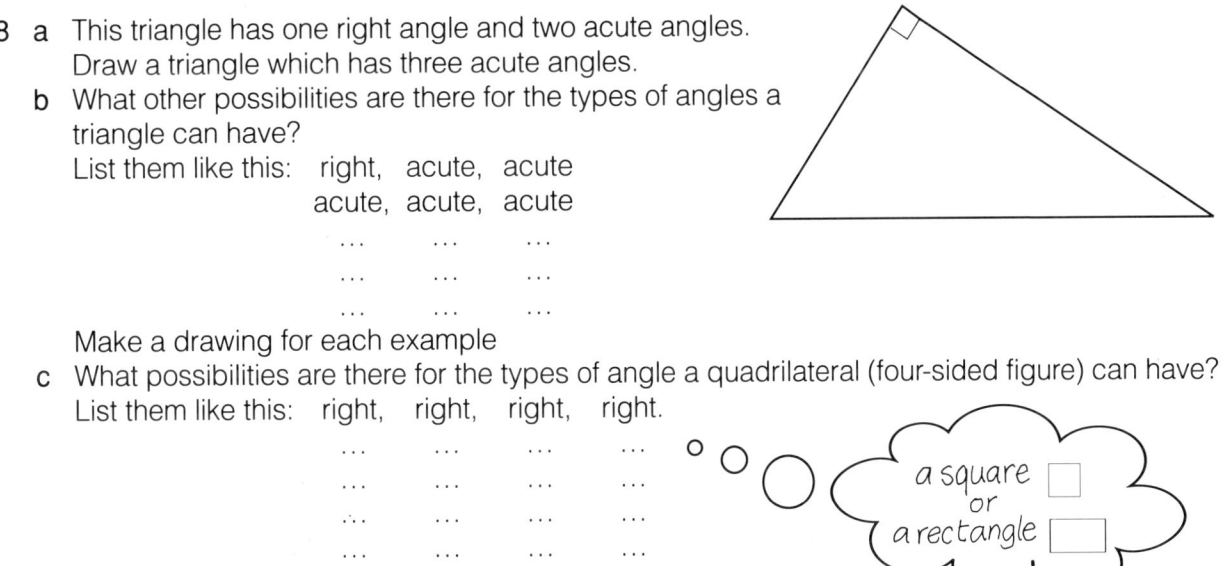

a square or a rectangle

Pot Black

No calculator, please

In Snooker there are 15 red balls and six different coloured balls.

Each red ball potted scores 1 point.
This is what the colours score.

Yellow (Y)	Green (G)	Brown (Br)	Blue (Bl)	Pink (P)	Black (B)
2 points	3 points	4 points	5 points	6 points	7 points

1 How many points do you score if you pot:

R → Br → R → P

2 How many points do you score if you pot:

R → P → R → B → R → B → R → Y → R

Here is a *break* of 23.

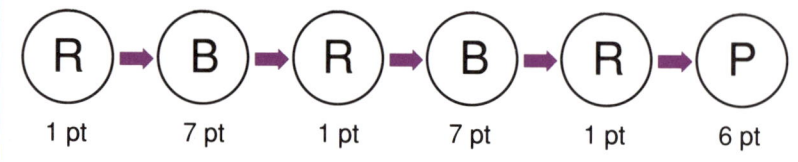

R → B → R → B → R → P
1 pt   7 pt   1 pt   7 pt   1 pt   6 pt

Total Break
23 points

3 Write down a break of 18.

You must pot a red ball before you pot a colour. The colours are put back on the table, but not the reds.

4 Write down a break of 30.

5 Write down a break of 50.

Pot Black

6 Which colour was potted last in this break?

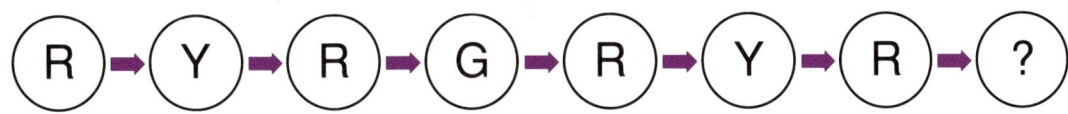

R → Y → R → G → R → Y → R → ?

Total Break 16 points

7 In this break the same colour was potted 3 times. What was it?

R → ? → R → ? → R → ? → R

Total Break 22 points

8 When there are no reds left on the table the other colours have to be potted in this order:

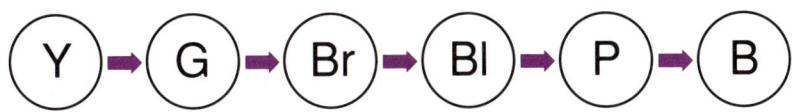

Y → G → Br → Bl → P → B

How many points are scored, altogether if all six colours are potted?

THE FINAL

George Pinter and Jackie Shaw have reached the Pot Black final.

9 This is George Pinter's score card.
How many points did he score?

Visit	George Pinter	Break
1st	R	1
2nd	R → Y → R → Bl → R	
3rd	R → P → R → ?	14
4th	R → G → R → B	12
5th	Y → G	
6th	P	

10 Jackie Shaw's score card is not shown.
These are the breaks he made in his six visits to the table.
The numbers in brackets show how many balls were potted.
8 (2); 7 (3); 12 (5); 7 (3); 9 (2); 7 (1)
a Write out a score card like George Pinter's to show which balls he potted.
b Is there more than one possible way to complete the card?
Explain your answer.

If he stops, can you?

Stopping distances.

1. How fast is the motorbike travelling?

The shortest stopping distance at 60 km/h can be shown like this.

| thinking distance 12 metres | braking distance 18 metres |

2. What is the shortest total stopping distance for the motorbike at 60km/h?

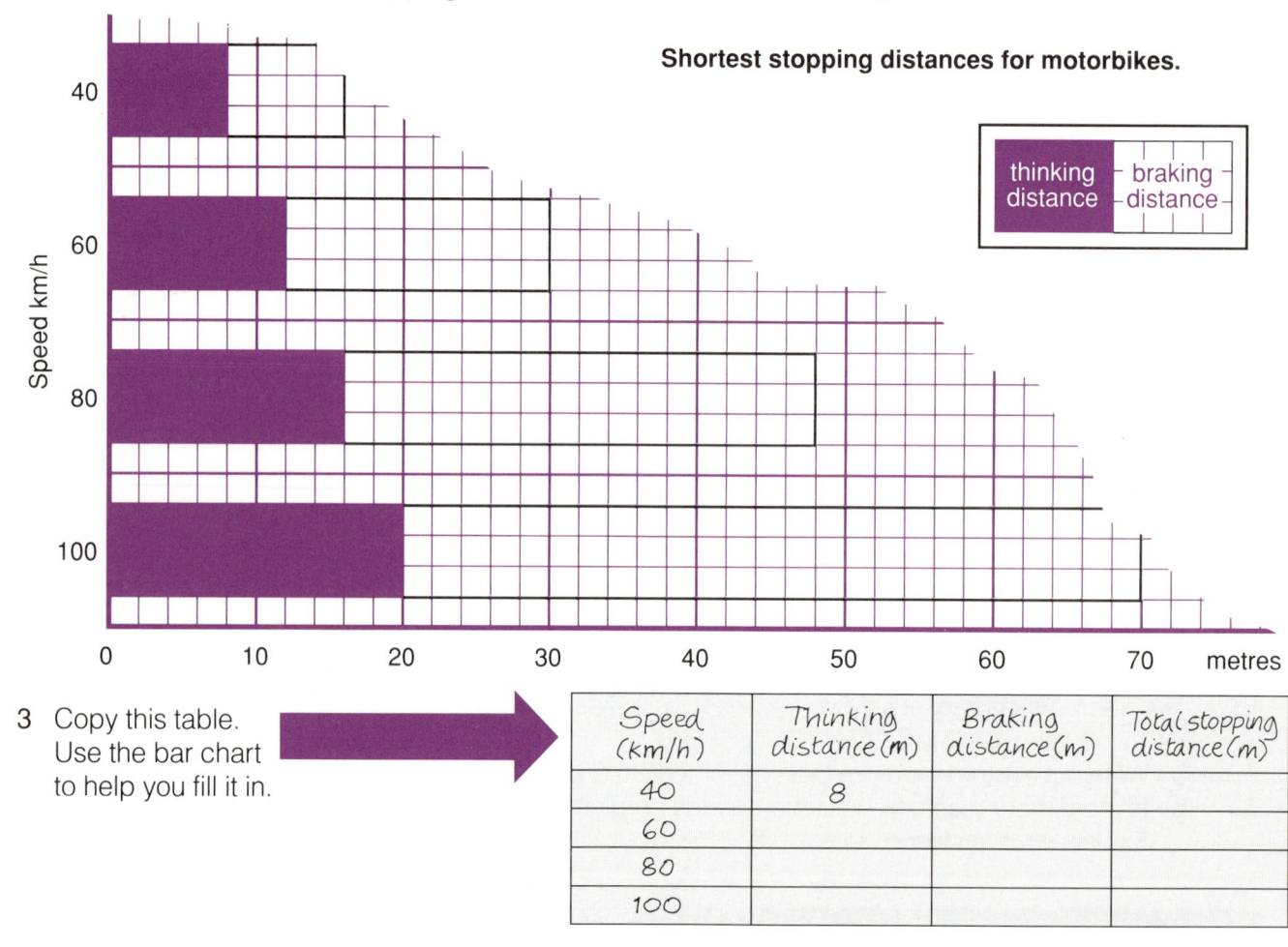

Shortest stopping distances for motorbikes.

3. Copy this table. Use the bar chart to help you fill it in.

Speed (km/h)	Thinking distance (m)	Braking distance (m)	Total stopping distance (m)
40	8		
60			
80			
100			

If he stops, can you?

MOTORBIKE ACCIDENTS.

Bar chart of the number of serious motorbike accidents during 1990

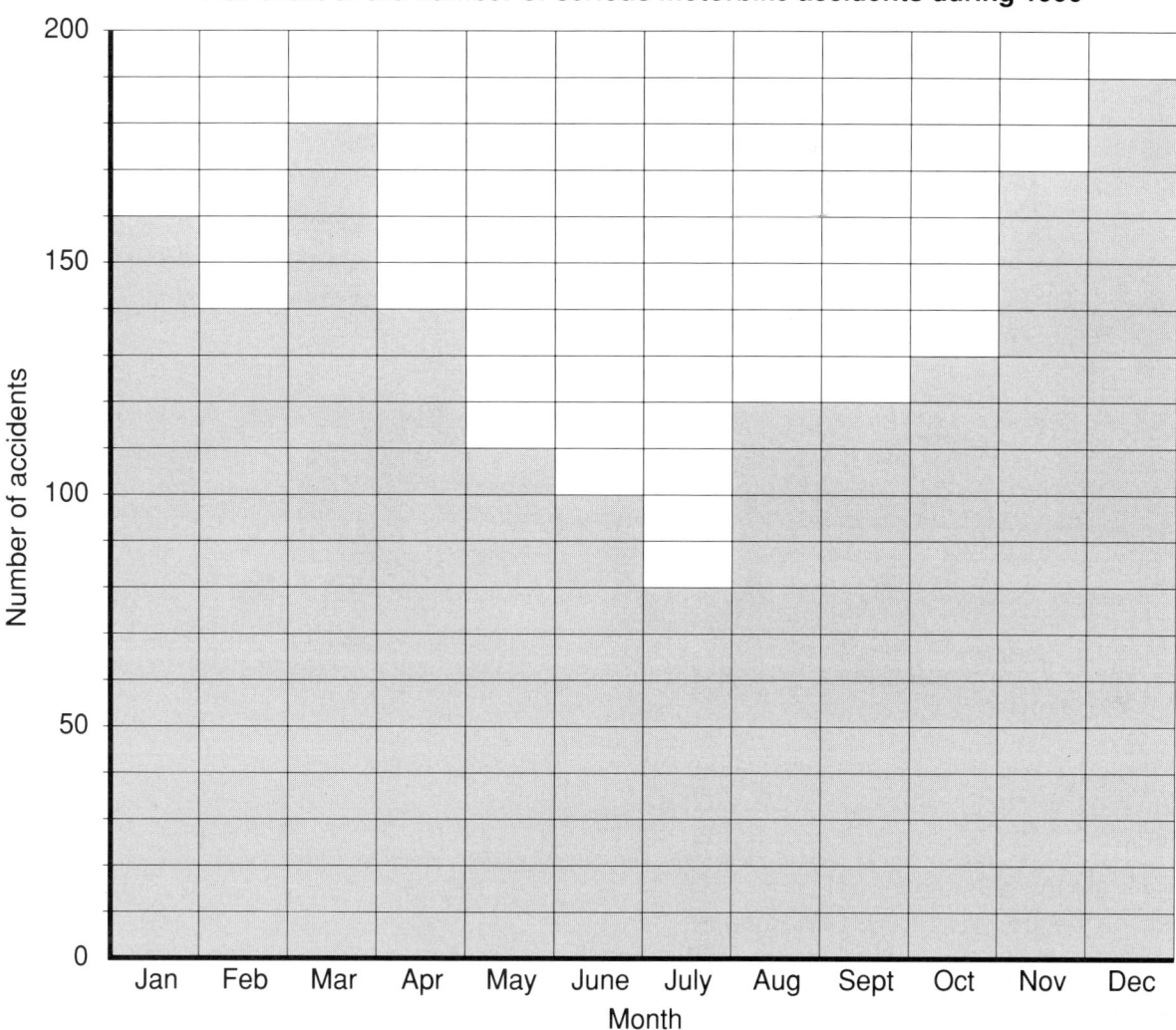

4 a In which month was there most accidents?
   b How many were there?

5 Copy this table. Fill it in.

Month	Jan	Feb	Mar	Apr	May	June	July	Aug	Sept	Oct	Nov	Dec
Number of accidents	160											

This table shows the number of riders killed during 1990.

Month	Jan	Feb	Mar	Apr	May	June	July	Aug	Sept	Oct	Nov	Dec
Number killed	60	30	80	20	10	10	20	30	20	20	40	50

6 How many riders were killed in February?

7 Draw your own bar chart to show the number of riders killed each month.

8 Why do you think so many riders were killed between November and March?

Work Experience

Emma and Pardip are on two weeks work experience.
For the first week they are at Price's bakery in Bradford.

1 Find on the map where Emma and Pardip live. Who lives nearer the Training Centre, Emma or Pardip?

2 This is the route Pardip takes to the Training Centre: Well St ➡ Leeds Road ➡ Vicar Lane ➡ Burnett St ➡ Peckover St. Measure (to the nearest cm) how far this is on the map.

3 How far does Pardip have to walk to get to the Training Centre:
   a in metres?
   b in kilometres?

Emma arranges to meet Pardip at the Car Park. They go to the Training Centre together.

4 Work out how far (to the nearest kilometre) Emma walks altogether.

5 Can you find a better route for Emma and Pardip? Write down where they meet and how far they each have to walk.

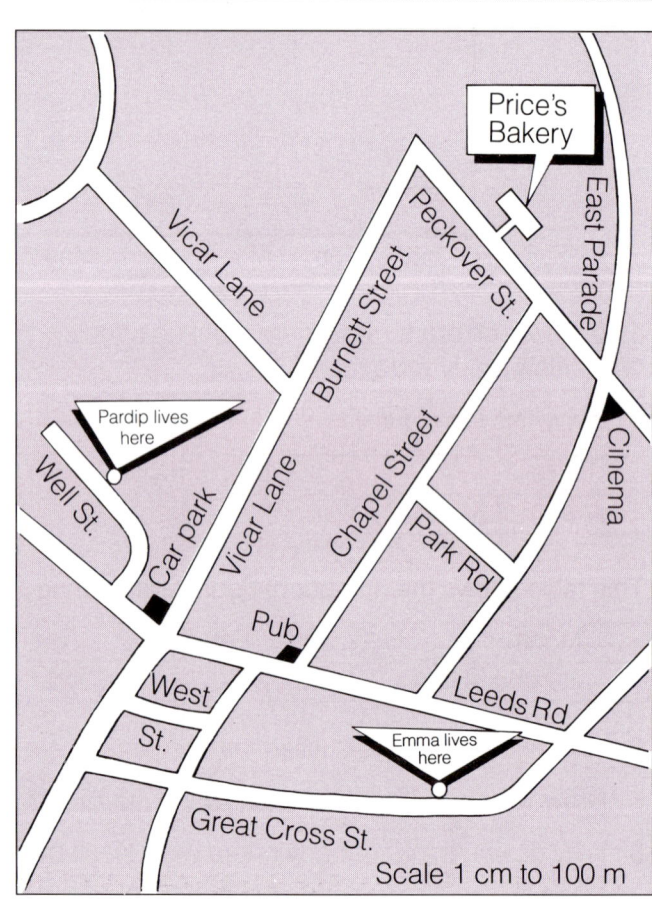

Scale 1 cm to 100 m

Work Experience

Next week Emma and Pardip are on work experience with a Leeds caterer.
They are providing a meal in Chapeltown.

6 The caterer hires her crockery from a firm in Dewsbury.
   Write down a route from Leeds to Chapeltown stopping off at Dewsbury.

7 a Using string, measure the distance on the map to the nearest $\frac{1}{2}$ centimetre.
   b How far is your route to the nearest kilometre?

Pardip's mum gives Emma and Pardip a lift to Chapeltown to meet the caterer.

8 a Write down a route they can take using mostly motorways.
   b How far is this route?

The caterer gives Emma and Pardip a lift back home, calling at Dewsbury on the way.

9 a Choose a route for them to take.
      Write down which roads they travel along.
   b How far do they travel altogether in the day?

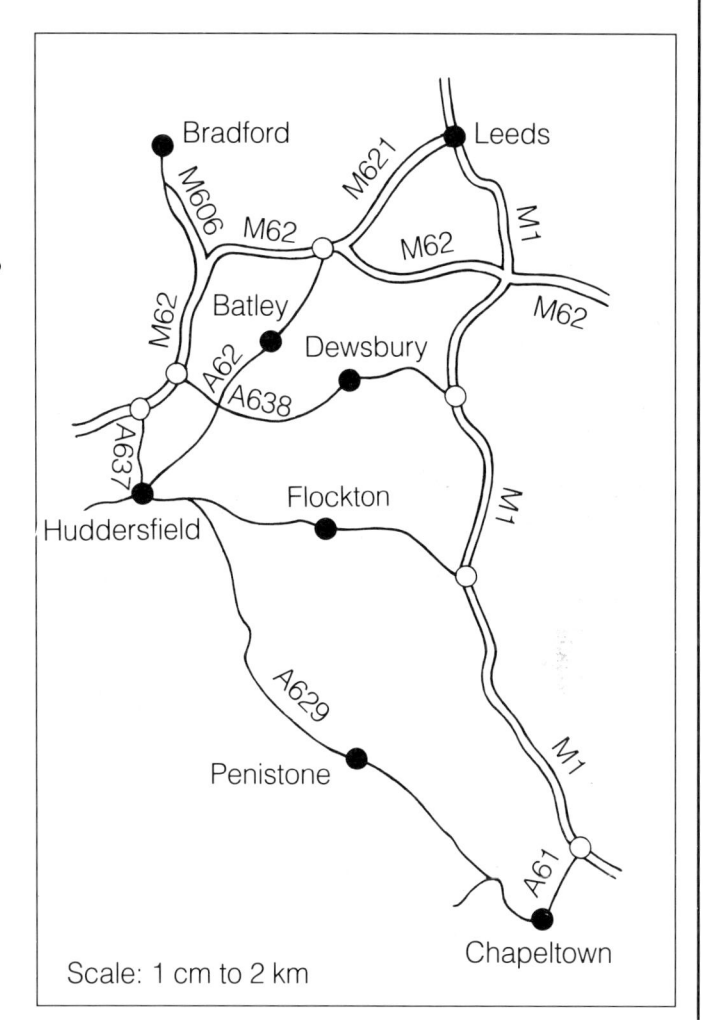

Scale: 1 cm to 2 km

PASTRY ROUND

10 The caterer also delivers cakes and pastries to each of the towns on the map. She has two vans.
   Plan a delivery route for each van.
   How far does each van travel?

Shapes on Screen

Mica has written this computer program. She makes an arrow move on the screen.

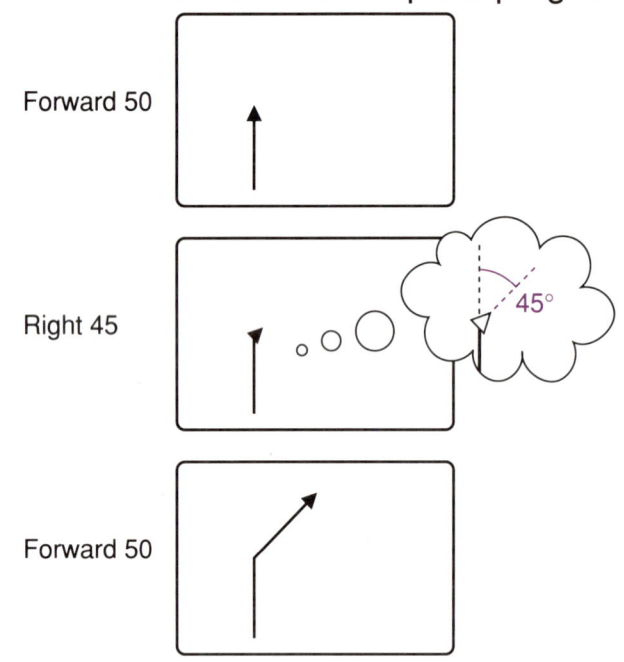

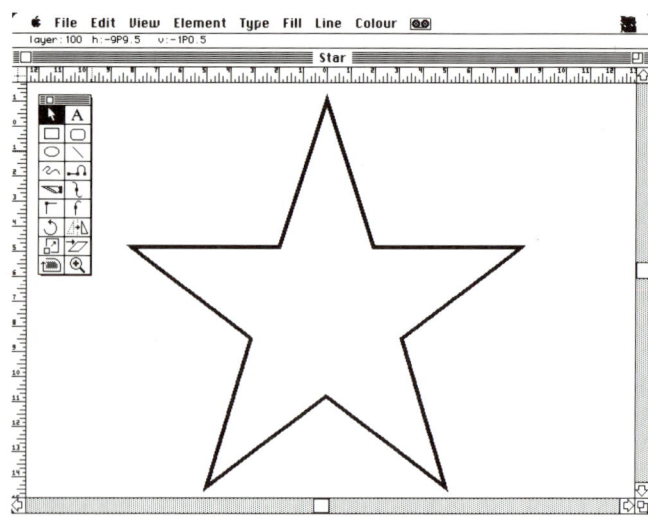

Forward 50

Right 45 (45°)

Forward 50

1. What is the effect of the instruction RIGHT 45?

2. On squared paper sketch the effect of each of these programs.

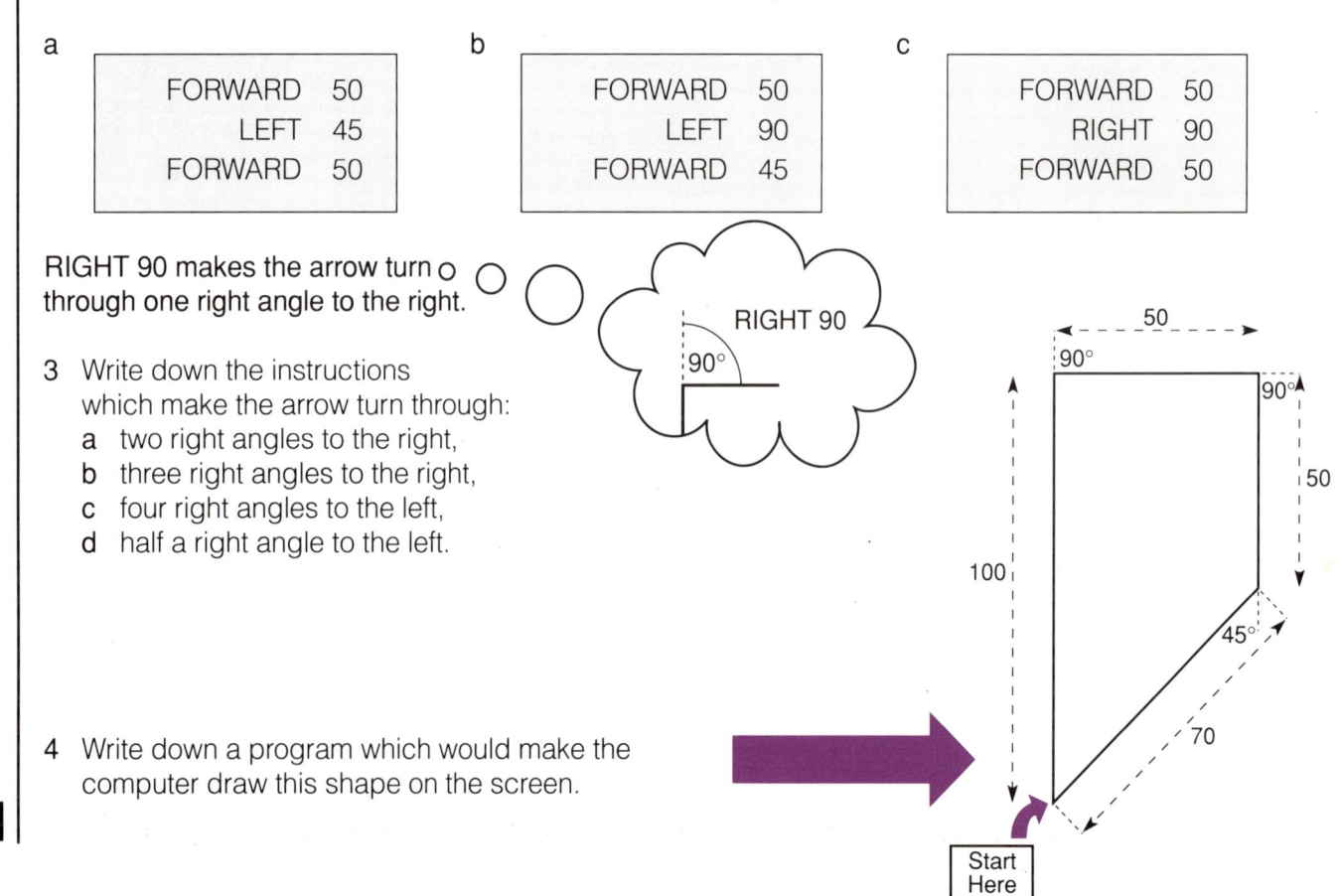

a
```
FORWARD  50
LEFT     45
FORWARD  50
```

b
```
FORWARD  50
LEFT     90
FORWARD  45
```

c
```
FORWARD  50
RIGHT    90
FORWARD  50
```

RIGHT 90 makes the arrow turn through one right angle to the right.

RIGHT 90 (90°)

3. Write down the instructions which make the arrow turn through:
   a. two right angles to the right,
   b. three right angles to the right,
   c. four right angles to the left,
   d. half a right angle to the left.

4. Write down a program which would make the computer draw this shape on the screen.

(Shape dimensions: 50, 90°, 90°, 50, 45°, 70, 100, Start Here)

24

Shapes on Screen

5 Write down the computer program needed to draw these on the screen.
You will need a protractor to measure the angles.

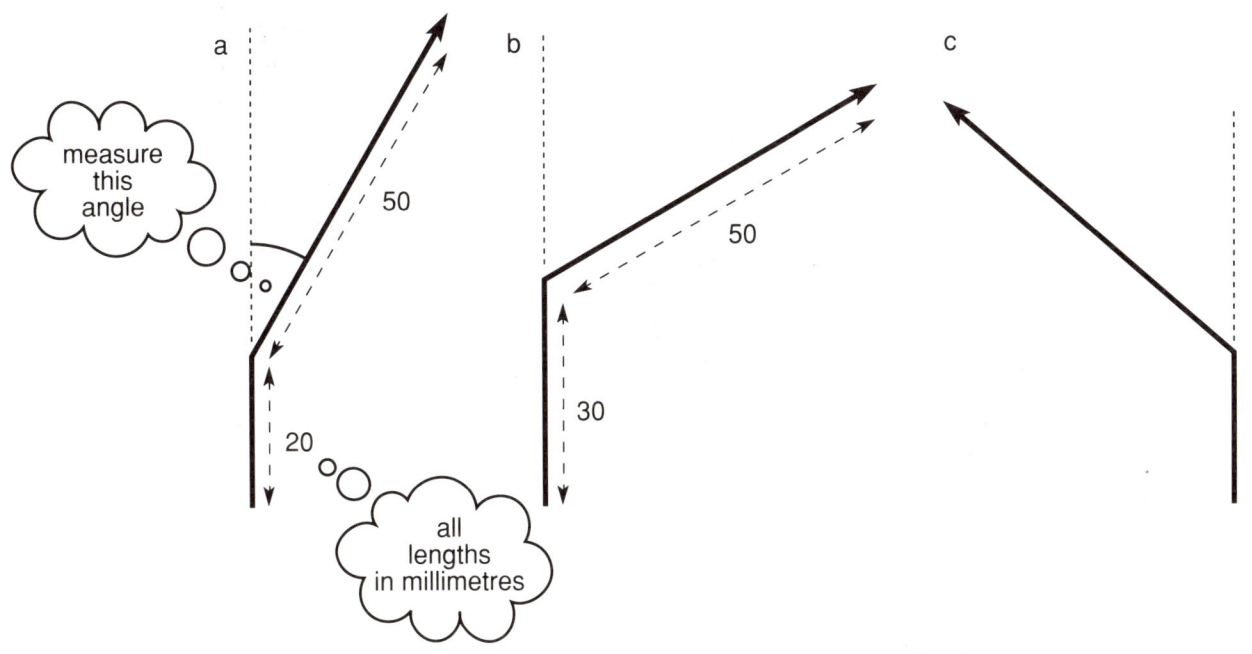

a (measure this angle) 50 20

b 50 30

c

all lengths in millimetres

6 Make **accurate drawings** of what the computer would show on the screen for these programs:

a
```
FORWARD  30
   RIGHT  60
FORWARD  60
```

b
```
FORWARD  40
   RIGHT  20
FORWARD  60
```

c
```
FORWARD  50
    LEFT  60
FORWARD  60
```

d
```
FORWARD  40
    LEFT  20
FORWARD  60
```

7 Mica writes this program to draw another shape.
   a Make an accurate drawing of what the computer would show on the screen for Mica's program.
   b What name is given to this shape?

```
FORWARD   60
   RIGHT 120
FORWARD   60
   RIGHT 120
FORWARD   60
```

COMPUTER SHAPES

This program will give a regular pentagon. ➡

```
FORWARD  50
    LEFT 72
FORWARD  50
    LEFT 72
FORWARD  50
    LEFT 72
FORWARD  50
    LEFT 72
FORWARD  50
```

8 Write a program to draw:
   a a square,
   b a regular hexagon,
   c a regular octagon,
   d a five-pointed star.
   Check your programs by drawing, or by using a computer.

25

Paper Folds

You need at least 2 strips of paper about 30 cm long.

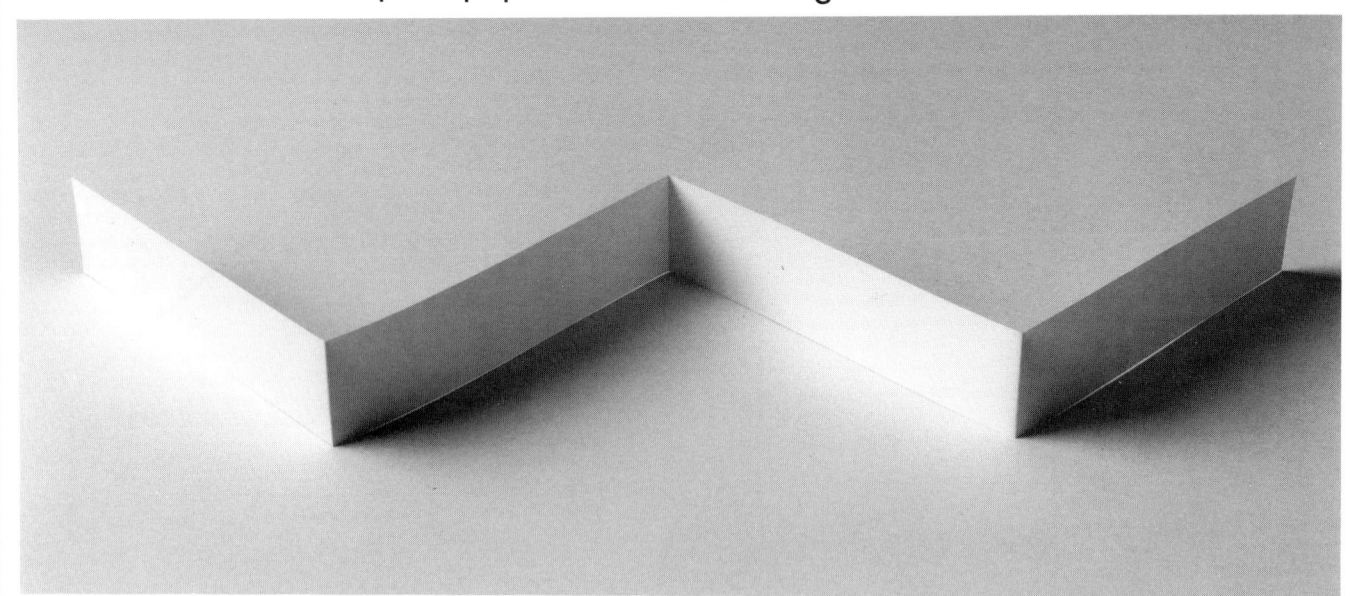

Fold one of the strips in half.

1. a How many thicknesses of paper do you have?
   b How many creases have you made?

Fold your strip in half again.

2. a How many thicknesses of paper are there now?
   b How many creases have you made altogether?

3. Copy the table and fill it in for 1 and 2 folds.

Number of folds	1	2	3	4	5	6	7	8	9	10
Number of thicknesses	2									
Number of creases										

4. a Fold the strip in half a third and fourth time.
   b Count the number of thicknesses and creases each time.

5. Complete the columns in the table for 3 and 4 folds.

6. Now guess for 5 folds:
   a how many thicknesses there would be?
   b how many creases there would be?

7. Check your answers by folding the paper in half again.
   a How many thicknesses are there?
   b How many creases have you made altogether?

Paper Folds

8   Were your guesses correct?
    If not try to find out why.

9   Complete the table for 5 folds.

10 Copy the 'number of the thicknesses' list from your table like this:

    ## 2, 4, 8, 16, 32, ...

11 Describe, in words, any patterns that you can find in the numbers.

12 What are the next two numbers after 32 in the pattern? Write them in your table.

13 Copy the 'number of creases' list from your table like this:

    ## 1, 3, 7, 15, 31, ...

14 Describe, in words, any patterns that you can find in the numbers.

15 What are the next two numbers after 31 in the pattern? Write them in your table.

16 Complete both rows of your table following the number patterns carefully.

17 Describe in words the connection between the number of creases and the number of thicknesses each time.

18 Imagine the paper was folded in half 10 times.
    a How many thicknesses would you expect?
    b How many creases would you expect?
    c What would your answers be if you folded your paper in half 20 times?

RECTANGLES

Take a new strip of paper.
Fold it in half then unfold it.

19 How many rectangles are there?

20 Keep folding the strip as you did before.
    Each time write down the number of rectangles there are.
    Investigate the patterns in these numbers.

27

Lanbourne Pottery

Jackie and Tricia work in Lanbourne Pottery.

Jackie gets 75p for each mug she paints.
Tricia gets 35p for each dinner set she packs.

1. How much does Jackie earn for painting:
   a 2 mugs?
   b 5 mugs?
   c 10 mugs?

2. How much does Tricia earn for packing:
   a 2 dinner sets?
   b 5 dinner sets?
   c 10 dinner sets?

3. On Monday Jackie earned £24.
   How many mugs did she paint?

4. On Monday Tricia earned £22.75.
   How many dinner sets did she pack?

These are the job cards for Jackie and Tricia.

| Week ending 31st January Jackie Shaw ||
Day	Number of mugs painted
Monday	24
Tuesday	28
Wednesday	33
Thursday	35
Friday	22

| Week ending 31st January Tricia Stevens ||
Day	Number of sets packed
Monday	65
Tuesday	32
Wednesday	48
Thursday	46
Friday	41

5. Work out how much Jackie earned in the week.
6. How much did Tricia earn in the week?

Lanbourne Pottery

In February the pottery introduced a bonus scheme.

These are the new pay rates.

Painting Mugs	
Number per day	Rate per mug
First 20 mugs	75p
Each additional mug over 20	95p

Packing dinner sets	
Number per day	Rate per set
First 40 sets	35p
Each additional set over 40	50p

7 On Monday Jackie painted 21 mugs.
   For how many mugs was she paid:
   a 75p per mug?
   b 95p per mug?

8 How much did Jackie earn altogether on Monday?

9 Copy Jackie's pay card.
   Fill it in.

Week ending 7th February Jackie Shaw	Mon	Tues	Wed	Thur	Fri
Number of mugs painted	21	30	32	34	25
Number painted at 75p each	20				
Number painted at 95p each	1				
Total pay	£15.95				

10 How much did Jackie earn in the week?

11 On Monday Tricia packed 43 dinner sets.
    For how many dinner sets was she paid:
    a 35p per set?
    b 50p per set?

12 How much did Tricia earn altogether on Monday?

13 This is Tricia's pay card.
    Work out the missing entries.

Week ending 7th February Tricia Stevens	Mon	Tue	Wed	Thur	Fri
Number of dinner sets packed	43		42		
Number packed at 35p each	40				
Number packed at 50p each	3	2	2	3	
Total pay		£15.00	£15.00	£15.50	£17.50

29

Sun Seeking

Clacton

The graph shows the average number of hours of sunshine per day in Clacton.

1. Which month has:
   a. the **highest** average number of hours of sunshine per day?
   b. the **lowest** average number of hours of sunshine per day?

2. Which months have:
   a. an average of more than 5 hours sunshine per day?
   b. an average of less than 3 hours sunshine per day?

3. Which month has 5.6 hours of sunshine per day?

4. List the average number of hours of sunshine per day for each month.

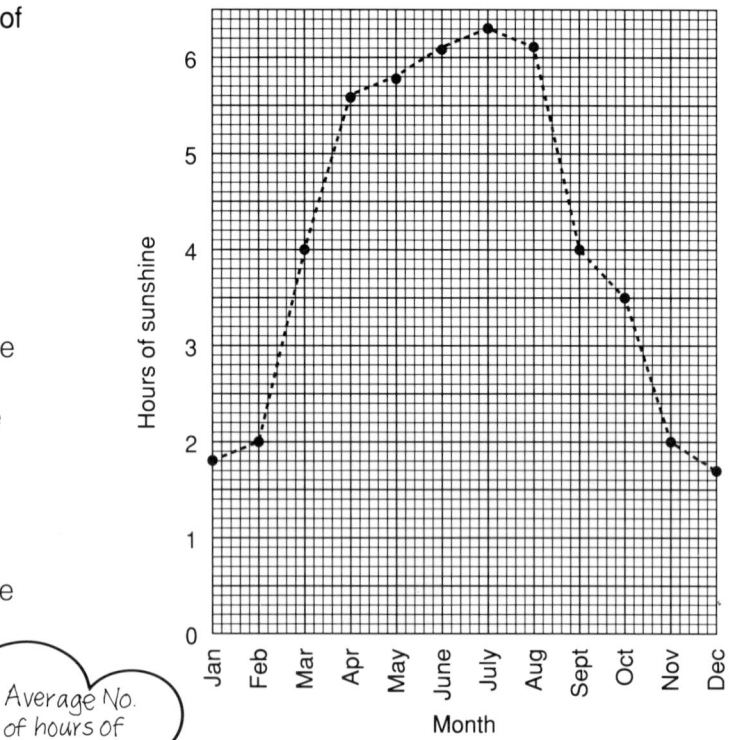

Month	Average No. of hours of sunshine per day
Jan	1.8
Feb	2
March	

Sun Seeking

Costa Blanca

The graph shows the average number of hours of sunshine per day on the Costa Blanca.

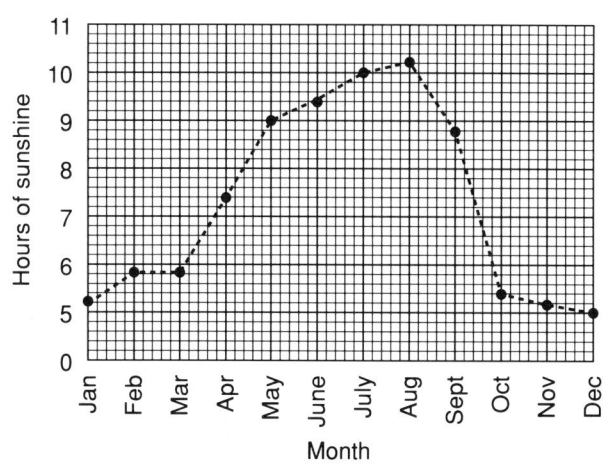

5 What is the average number of hours of sunshine per day in August?

6 a Which month has the **lowest** average number of hours of sunshine per day?
  b How many hours of sunshine does it have?

7 Make a list like the one for question 4, of the average number of hours of sunshine per day for each month.

Costa del Sol

This table shows the average number of hours of sunshine per day on the Costa del Sol.

Month	Jan	Feb	Mar	Apr	May	June	July	Aug	Sept	Oct	Nov	Dec
Average number of hours of sunshine per day	5.8	6.3	7.8	9.0	10.1	10.7	11.4	11.6	8.7	6.8	6.0	5.4

8 Draw the sunshine graph for the Costa del Sol.

9 Which of the 3 resorts would you choose for the sunniest holiday in July?

10 How many hours of sunshine per day would you expect?

What's it worth?

Mike Baxter writes for the Evening Herald.
Every month he publishes a price guide for local second-hand cars.

| Herald Guide to used cars Prices quoted are **average** prices for the area ||||||
Make of car	1985	1986	1987	1988	1989
Vauxhall Cavalier	£3325	£4720	£6000	£7400	
Rover 216	£3510	£5500	£6800	£7500	
Ford Escort	£3800	£4900	£5500	£6400	
Peugeot 205	£4330	£5200	£6130	£6800	
Nissan Sunny	£3335	£4600		£6900	

To find the average price of a car Mike phones local garages and gets 10 quotes. He was quoted these prices for a 1988 Vauxhall Cavalier.

£7425 £7500 £7135 £7650 £7510
£7450 £7200 £7300 £7370 £7430

1 What was the highest price Mike was quoted?

2 What was the lowest price he was quoted?

3 What is the total cost of the 10 Cavaliers?

4 What average price should Mike print?
   (Check your answer in the Herald Guide.)

He was quoted these prices for a 1987 Nissan Sunny.

£5420 £5950 £5500 £5800 £6100
£5690 £5995 £5985 £6200 £5950

5 What is the total cost of the 10 Nissan Sunnys?

6 What price should Mike print in the Herald Guide?

7 How many of the prices quoted to him were:
   a above the average?
   b below the average?

8 What was the range of prices quoted for the Nissan Sunny?

32

What's it worth?

Dean and Emma are looking for a second-hand car.
They have £5500 to spend.

9 Look at the Herald Guide. Write down which cars have a price less than £5500.

Dean and Emma decide on an Escort. They go to Murray's.

MURRAY'S CAR SALES

1987 (E) FORD ESCORT 1.4L 5-door Hatch, medium blue with grey patterned cloth trim, fitted radio/cassette, rear seat belts, splendid condition.....£5695

1987 FORD ESCORT 1300. In showroom condition or the year, undersealed and finished in glacier white with black coachwork. An excellent buy at £5500

1987 FORD ESCORT. Finished in Venetian red, with tan cloth interior. Offered at £5315

1986 ESCORT XR3i Wide wheels, new engine, stereo, long MOT. Offered at £5295

1986 FORD ESCORT. Metallic brown, low mileage, a real bargain at only £4495

1985 FORD ESCORT. 4 door, orange with black interior, economical car in good condition for year. A good buy at £3595

1985 ESCORT 1.6GL high mileage £3480

10 Which Escort at Murray's is exactly the price shown in the Herald Guide?

11 How much over the price in the Herald Guide are Murray's asking for the blue 1987 Escort 1.4L?

12 List all the cars from Murray's that Dean and Emma can afford.

13 Dean likes the 1986 Escort XR3i. Is it above or below the price in the Herald Guide?

14 Emma wants the brown 1986 Escort. Is it above or below the price in the Herald Guide?

15 Which car would you buy? Why?

Return Ticket

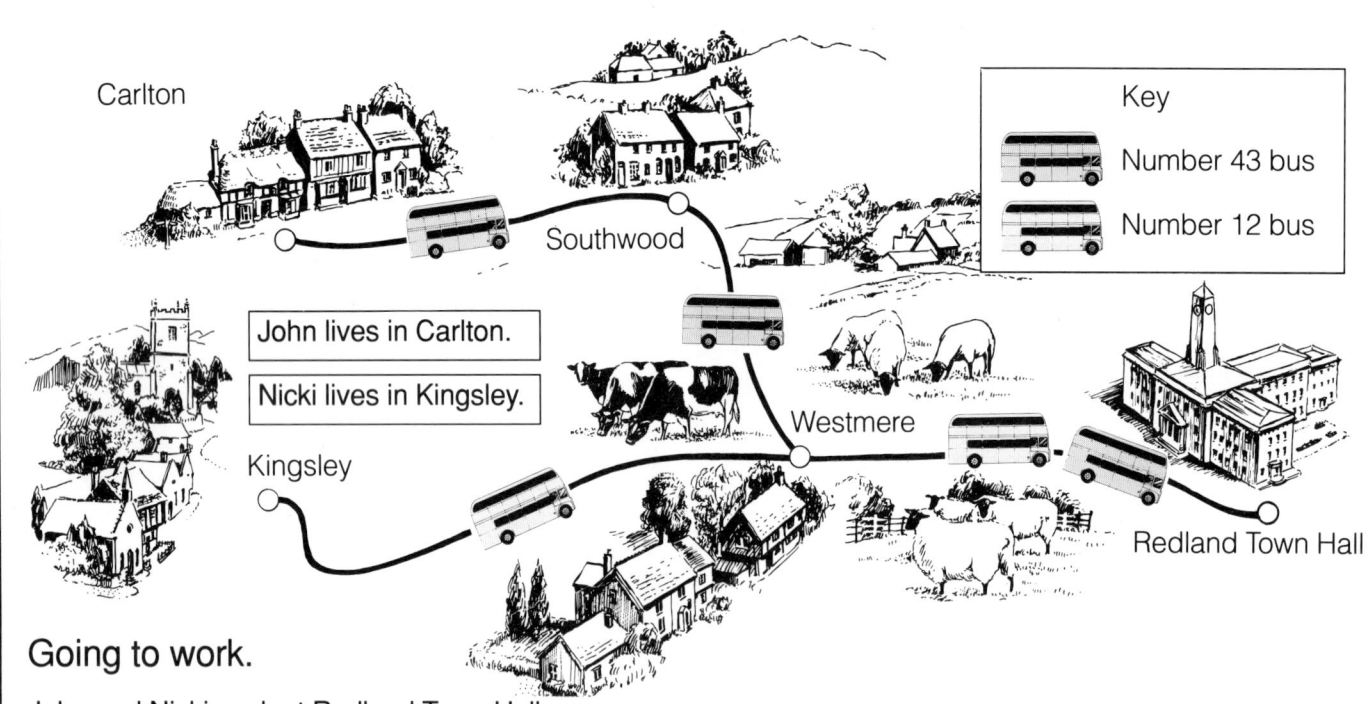

Carlton — Southwood — Westmere — Redland Town Hall

Kingsley

Key
- Number 43 bus
- Number 12 bus

John lives in Carlton.
Nicki lives in Kingsley.

Going to work.

John and Nicki work at Redland Town Hall.
They travel to work by bus.

1. John catches the number 43 bus. Which bus does Nicki catch?

2. Between which 2 places do the buses follow the same route?

Here is the early morning timetable for the number 43 bus.

| Leaves Carlton | 6.05 | 6.35 | 7.05 | 7.25 | 7.45 | 8.05 | 8.17 | 8.29 | 8.41 | 8.53 | 9.05 | 9.20 | 9.35 | 9.50 | and then every 30 mins |
| Arrives Redland Town Hall | 6.32 | 7.02 | 7.32 | 7.52 | 8.12 | 8.32 | 8.44 | 8.56 | 9.08 | 9.20 | 9.32 | 9.47 | 10.02 | 10.17 | |

3. What time is the first bus from Carlton?

4. How many buses are there between 6 a.m. and 7 a.m.?

5. Copy this table. Fill it in.

Time	6a.m.–7a.m.	7a.m.–8a.m.	8a.m.–9a.m.	9a.m.–10a.m.	10a.m.–11a.m.	11a.m.–12 noon
Number of buses from Carlton						

6. In which hour shown in the table do most buses leave Carlton?

7. a. John must be at work by 8.45 a.m. He wants to catch a bus **before** the peak hour starts. Which is the latest bus he should catch?
   b. What time does this get him to the Town hall?

8. If that bus is cancelled, will the next one get him there on time?

Return Ticket

This is the morning timetable for the number 12 bus.

9 What time does:
   a the first bus leave Kingsley?
   b the second bus leave Kingsley?

10 Write down the times of all the buses which leave Kingsley between 5 a.m. and 7 a.m.

11 How many buses leave Kingsley **per hour** between 5 a.m. and 7 a.m.?

12 How many buses leave Kingsley **per hour** during the morning peak period?

13 Nicki starts work at 8.30 a.m. Her bus journey takes 30 minutes. What is the latest bus she should catch?

Number 12 bus
Kingsley – Redland Town Hall

First bus: 5.04 a.m.

Morning
Buses leave every 20 minutes except during Peak Period.

Peak Period: 7.04 a.m. – 10.04 a.m.
Buses leave every 12 minutes.

Going home.

These are the bus times from Redland Town Hall during the evening peak period (4 p.m. – 6 p.m.)

14 In the peak period, how many buses **per hour** run:
   a on the 43 bus route?
   b on the 12 bus route?

Services From Redland Town Hall

Number 43 Route: Buses leave 4.05 p.m.
(to Carlton)   then every 15 minutes.

Number 12 Route :   Buses leave 4.04 p.m.
(to Kingsley)   then every 12 minutes.

John and Nicki finish work at 5 p.m.
They travel home together as far as Westmere.

15 How many buses per hour are there **altogether** to Westmere?

16 Do you think John and Nicki are more likely to catch a 43 bus or a 12 bus? Why?

35

Pop Prints

Barbara sees this advert in the *Melody Express*.

Pop Prints Ltd

Big colour prints of your favourite stars

Poster £3

T-shirt £3.80

Velour Sweatshirt £12.00

Silver necklace £6.20

Jumbo Badge £1.60

Special introductory offer

10% (10p in the £) **off printed prices if all orders sent before 31st May.**

1. What is the **percentage** reduction in the introductory offer?

2. a How much would Barbara save on a poster?
   b How much would she pay for the poster?

3. Copy this table. Fill it in.

Item	Savings (10%)	Offer Price
Poster	30p	£2.70
Jumbo Badge		
Necklace		
T-shirt		
Sweatshirt		

4. a How much would Barbara save if she bought a poster and a T-shirt **before 31st May**?
   b What would they cost her altogether?

Pop Prints

Barbara got this advert with her order.

> Discounts for large orders from **Pop Prints Ltd**
> *Why not send an order for yourself and your friends?*
> We give these discounts:
>
> | Order value | Over £40 | Over £50 | Over £60 |
> |---|---|---|---|
> | Discount | 20% | 25% | 30% |

5 a What percentage discount do Pop Prints give on an order of £46?
  b How much is this?

Barbara collected these orders from her friends in July.

Alan	1 poster	1 badge
Mary	1 poster	1 necklace
Ray	2 badges	
Sheila	2 necklaces	2 badges
Liz	2 sweatshirts	

6 Find the cost of each of her friend's orders.
  Write them down like this: Alan – £4.60, Mary …

7 What is the total cost of the order without discount?

8 What percentage discount would Barbara get?

9 a What would the saving be on the whole order?
  b What would be the **actual** cost of the order?

When Barbara found that the order was nearly £60 she ordered a badge, a poster and a necklace for herself to get the extra discount.

10 What was the total cost of all the orders without discount?

11 How much did Barbara actually send off for the order?

Using Maths

work with a friend

1 Sometimes you have to collect information yourself to solve problems.
  Together, discuss how you would solve each of these problems. For each one write down
  ★ what information you need to collect.
  ★ how you would collect the information
  ★ how you could use the information to solve the problem.

PROBLEM A
Find approximately how tall a tree is.

PROBLEM B
Find approximately how quickly the water in a river is flowing.

PROBLEM C
Estimate how many food trolleys the manager of a new supermarket needs to buy.

WATER ASSIGNMENT

You need a measuring jug, a ruler.
You also need to know and use these things:

1 litre = 1000 millilitres

1 litre of water takes up 1000 cm^3 of space, i.e. 10 cm x 10 cm x 10 cm of space.

1 litre of water weighs 1 kg

1000 litres of water weigh 1 tonne.

2 a This work will take you about 1 week and you will need to do much of it at home. You will need to measure and estimate.

   Find out approximately:
   i   how much water you drink each time you have a cup of tea,
   ii how much water you use each time you flush the loo,
   iii how much water you use each time you wash up the breakfast plates,
   iv how much water you use each time you have a bath.

   b Use your results in **a**, and any other estimates, to decide how much water, on average, you use each week at home.

Dream Kitchen

Barry is on work experience with a builder.

They are fitting new kitchen units. These are the units they can use.

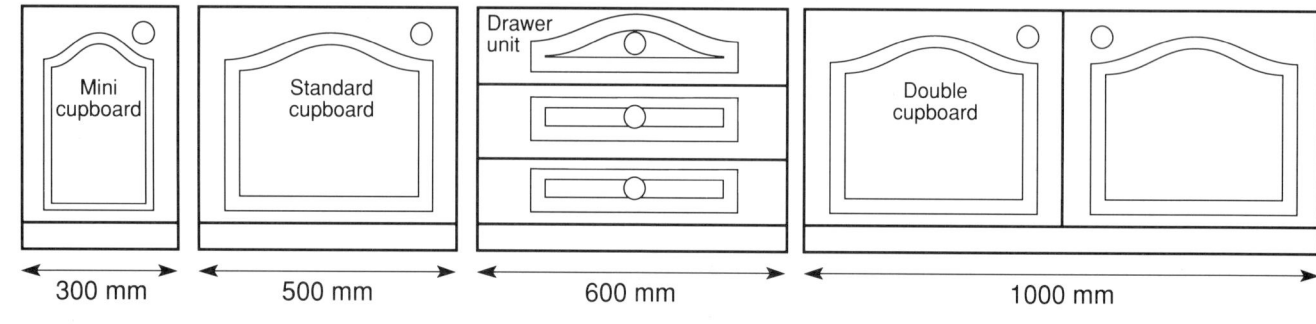

Mini cupboard	Standard cupboard	Drawer unit	Double cupboard
300 mm	500 mm	600 mm	1000 mm

1. Which unit is:
   a the widest?   b the narrowest?

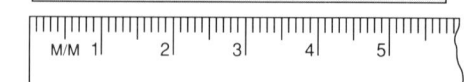

2. Copy this table. Fill it in.

Unit	Width (mm)	Width (cm)
Mini cupboard		
Standard cupboard		
Drawer unit		
Double cupboard		

Remember
10 millimetres = 1 centimetre
10 mm = 1 cm

The builder gives Barry this sketch plan of the kitchen.

3. Draw your own neat sketch plan of the kitchen. Show the position of the doors, sink unit and cooker.

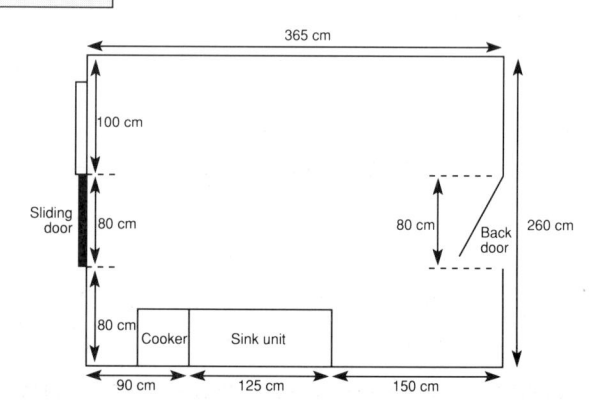

Dream Kitchen

Here are the cooker, the fridge and the washing machine.

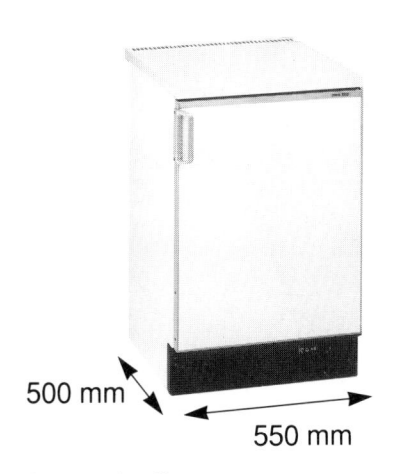

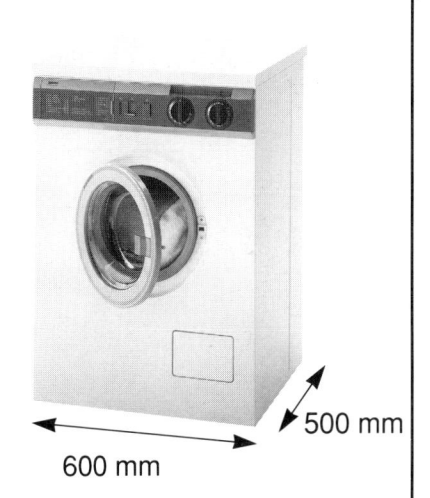

500 mm 600 mm   500 mm 550 mm   600 mm 500 mm

4   How wide in centimetres is: a   the cooker?
    b   the fridge?
    c   the washing machine?

Look at your sketch plan of the kitchen.

5   a   Which unit fits exactly into the space beside the cooker?
    b   Show this on your plan.

6   The washing machine is fitted next to the sink. Draw it on your plan.

7   How much space is left at the side of the washing machine:
    a   in centimetres?
    b   in millimetres?

8   a   Which two units fit exactly next to the washing machine?
    b   Show them on your plan.

9   How many double cupboard units could Barry and the builder fit along the wall opposite the sink?

10 What space would be left: a   in centimetres?
                               b   in millimetres?

11 If the fridge is fitted into this gap, how much room is left now?

12 Show on your sketch plan how the double cupboard units could be fitted along this wall.

PLAN YOUR KITCHEN

13 Make a sketch plan of your own kitchen.
    Mark on it the door, water and electric points.

14 Show the kitchen units you would fit, and where you would fit them. Remember you must include the cooker, fridge, washing machine and sink unit. All units are 50 cm deep.

41

Aircrash

A trident plane has had a mid-air collision.

The Airport Map will help you find out where it happened.
The circles on the map are 20 km apart.

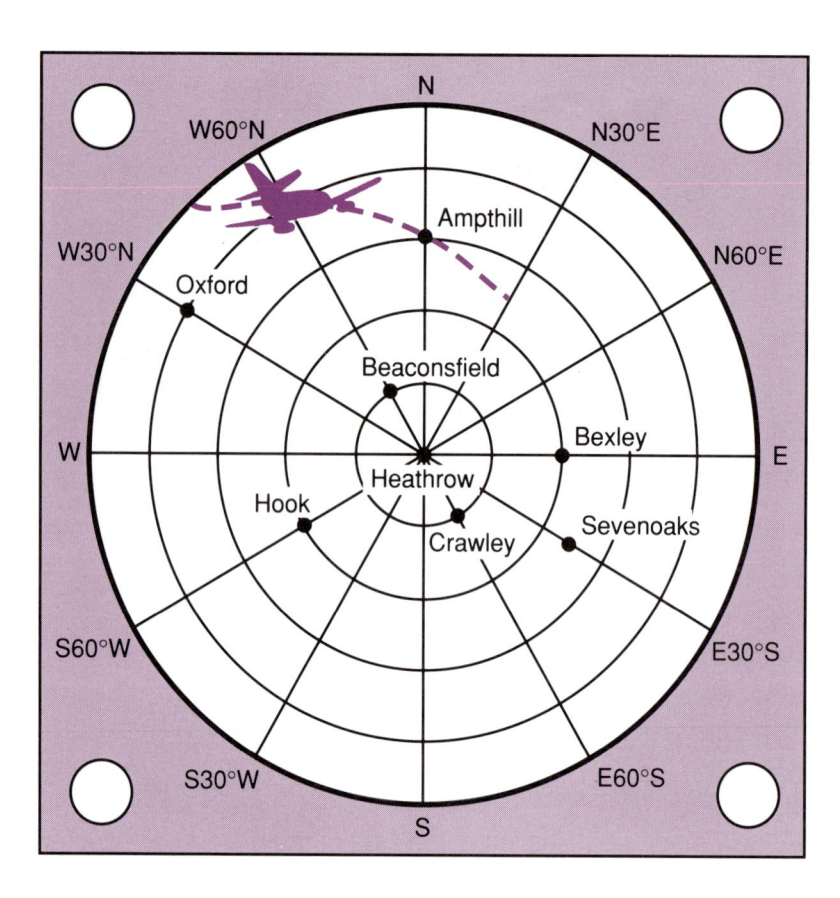

Key
Trident flight path

1 Which town is:
   a 20 km from Heathrow?
   b 80 km from Heathrow?

Imagine standing at Heathrow and facing East.
Turn 30° towards the South. You will be facing Sevenoaks. Sevenoaks is E 30°S of Heathrow.

2 Towards which town would you be facing if you turned another 30° to the south?

The direction you face to start with

The direction toward which you turn

3 Which town is:
   a W 30°N of Heathrow?
   b S 60°W of Heathrow?

4 Copy this table. Fill it in.

Town	Ampthill		Sevenoaks	Hook	Oxford	Beaconsfield	Crawley
Distance from Heathrow (km)		40					
Direction from Heathrow	N		E 30°S		W 30°N		

Aircrash

This is a record of the Trident's flight path.

Part of the flight path is shown on the Airport Map.

5 Which town was the Tident flying over at:
   a 08.02?
   b 08.08?

6 a Copy the Airport Map exactly, leaving out the towns. (You can trace it if you like.)
   b Use the table to plot the rest of the Trident's path on your map.

Last known position of Trident

Trident Flight Path Record		
Time	Distance from Heathrow (km)	Direction from Heathrow
08.00	80	W 60°N
08.02	60	N
08.04	50	N 30°E
08.06	50	N 60°E
08.08	40	E
08.10	40	E 60°S
08.12	20	S
08.14	20	S 30°W

At the time of the crash, radar was also tracking a D.C.10 and a Boeing 747.

These are their flight path records.

D.C.10 Flight Path Record		
Time	Distance from Heathrow (km)	Direction from Heathrow
08.04	80	S 30°W
08.06	70	S
08.08	60	E 60°S
08.10	60	E 30°S
08.12	60	N 60°E

Boeing 747 Flight Path Record		
Time	Distance from Heathrow (km)	Direction from Heathrow
08.06	80	W 30°N
08.08	60	W
08.10	50	S 60°W
08.12	40	S 30°W
08.14	20	S 30°W

7 Plot the flight path for each of these planes on your map.

8 One plane collided with the Trident. Which one do you think it was?

9 When the planes collided:
   a how far were they from Heathrow?
   b what was their bearing from Heathrow?
   c what time was it?

10 Mark on your map where the planes collided.

Phone Charges

Kate is having a barbecue. She is phoning to invite her friends.

These are the charges for local telephone calls.

	Time brought for 5p
Peak rate (9 a.m. – 1 p.m. Mon – Fri)	Up to 1 minute
Standard rate (8 a.m. – 9 a.m., 1 p.m. – 6 p.m. Mon – Fri)	Up to 2 minutes
Cheap Rate (after 6 p.m. and all weekends)	Up to 6 minutes

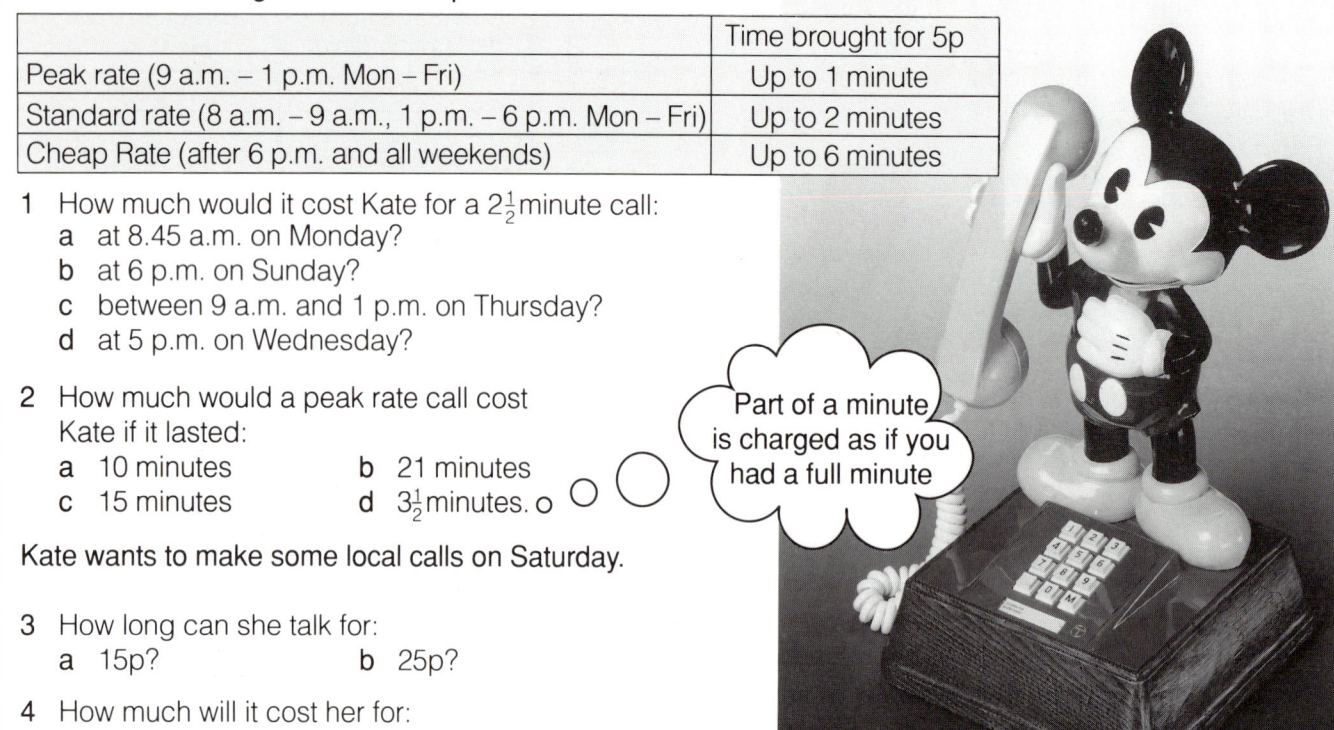

1. How much would it cost Kate for a $2\frac{1}{2}$ minute call:
   a. at 8.45 a.m. on Monday?
   b. at 6 p.m. on Sunday?
   c. between 9 a.m. and 1 p.m. on Thursday?
   d. at 5 p.m. on Wednesday?

2. How much would a peak rate call cost Kate if it lasted:
   a. 10 minutes
   b. 21 minutes
   c. 15 minutes
   d. $3\frac{1}{2}$ minutes.

Part of a minute is charged as if you had a full minute

Kate wants to make some local calls on Saturday.

3. How long can she talk for:
   a. 15p?
   b. 25p?

4. How much will it cost her for:
   a. a 1 minute call?
   b. a 5 minute call?
   c. a 6 minute call?
   d. a 9 minute call?

These are the first five friends Kate phoned to invite to the barbecue.

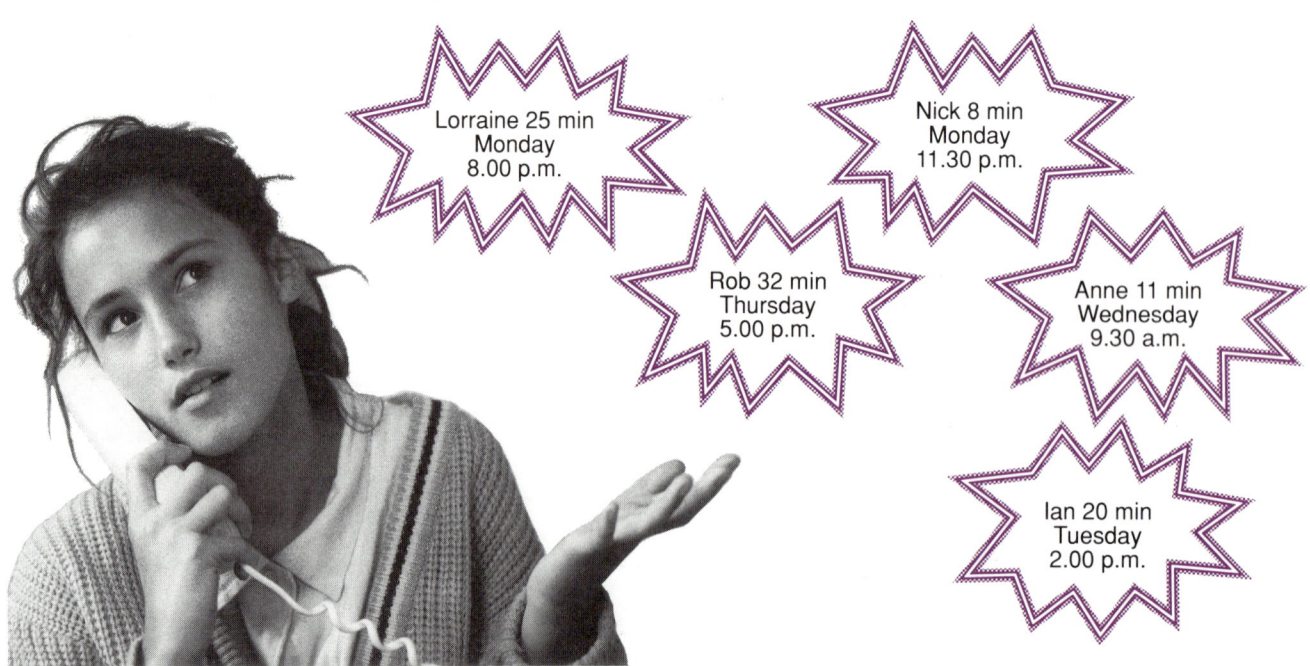

- Lorraine 25 min, Monday, 8.00 p.m.
- Nick 8 min, Monday, 11.30 p.m.
- Rob 32 min, Thursday, 5.00 p.m.
- Anne 11 min, Wednesday, 9.30 a.m.
- Ian 20 min, Tuesday, 2.00 p.m.

5. Work out how much it cost Kate to phone each of her five friends.

Phone Charges

She phoned the rest of her friends on Saturday.

6. Which of the three rates was Kate charged on Saturday?

7. The table shows how long Kate spent phoning each of her friends.
   Work out the cost of each call.

8. What did it cost her altogether to phone her 12 friends?

9. If VAT at 15% is added to this, what is the total cost?

Friend	Length of call
Jane	5 min
Pat	1 min 10s
Tony	6 min 4s
Scott	20 min
Debbie	9 min 20s
Sue	8 min
Alex	1 min 20s

Kate can find out the weather forecast for the day of the barbecue by ringing Weatherline.

10. What does it cost to phone Weatherline:
    a at peak rate?   b at cheap rate?

WEATHERLINE

For your Local weather Forecast just dial

Singing Weather Man   0898 765400
Weather in Rhyme   0898 765401
Weather in Brief   0898 765402

Charges Peak: 5p for 8 secs
Cheap: 5p for 12 secs

11. Each Weatherline message lasts for a different time.
    What would it cost Kate to phone each of these on Saturday?

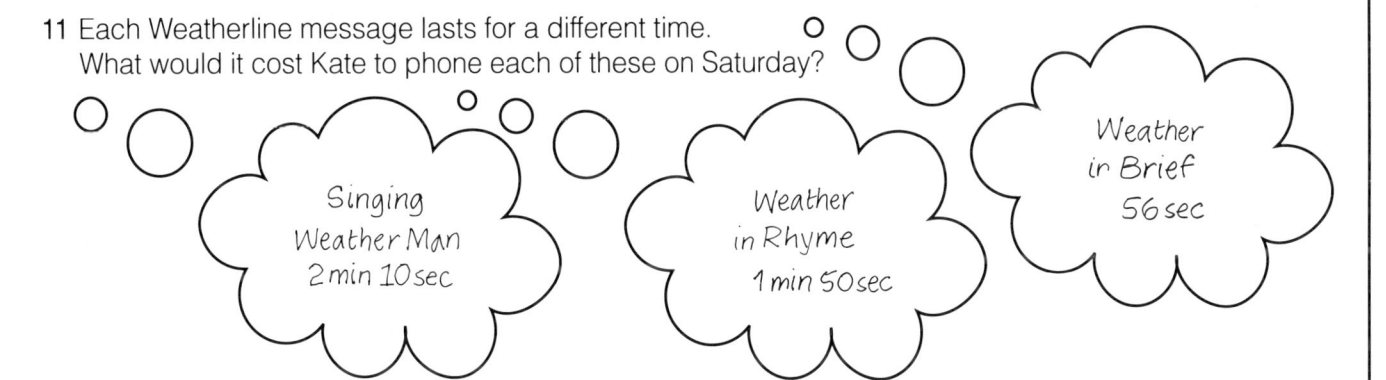

- Singing Weather Man 2 min 10 sec
- Weather in Rhyme 1 min 50 sec
- Weather in Brief 56 sec

SPECIAL SERVICES

12. Other telephone codes have special charge rates.
    Find out the charges for each of them.
    Make out a charge table for them.

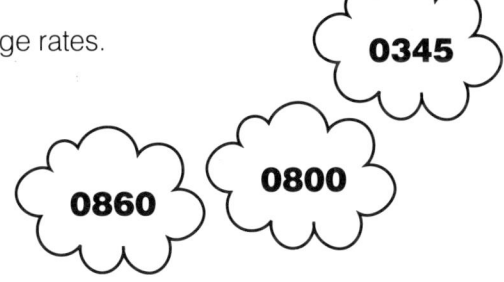

    0345
    0860
    0800

Hill Climb

The European Hill Climb Championship is in two stages.
The first stage is in Wales.

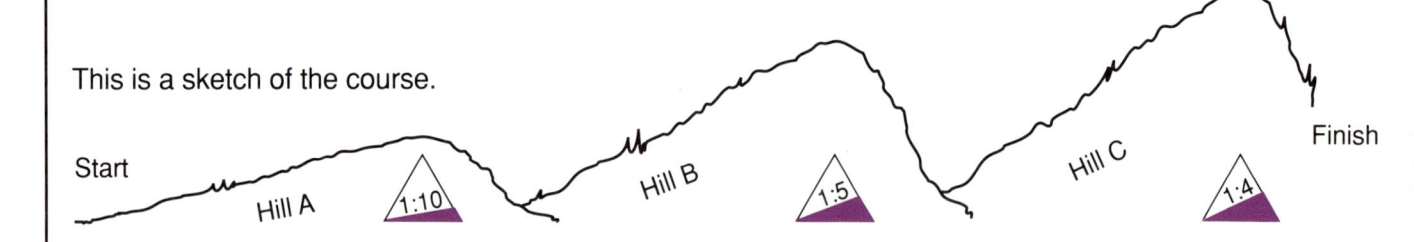

This is a sketch of the course.

Start — Hill A (1:10) — Hill B (1:5) — Hill C (1:4) — Finish

1. How many hills are there?

This is the sign for Hill A. (1:10)

(1:10) means you rise *1 metre* vertically for every *10 metres* you travel horizontally.

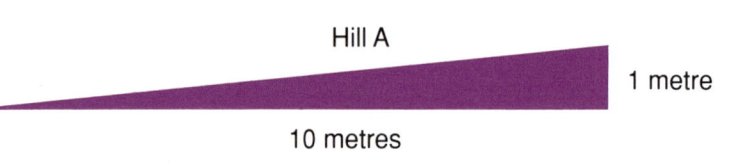

Hill A: 1 metre rise over 10 metres

2. How many metres do you have to travel horizontally to rise:
   a 2 metres vertically?
   b 3 metres vertically?

3. Copy this table. Fill it in.

	Hill A 1:10				Hill B 1:5				Hill C 1:4			
	1m / 10m				1m / 5m				1m / 4m			
Vertical rise (metres)	1	5	10	20	1	5	10	20	1	5	10	20
Horizontal distance (metres)	10	50			5				4			

4. Look at the last column in your table for each hill. Which hill has:
   a the steepest slope?
   b the gentlest slope?

Hill Climb

The second stage of the Championship is in Germany.

German hill signs look like this.

20% means you rise *20 metres* vertically for every *100 metres* you travel horizontally.

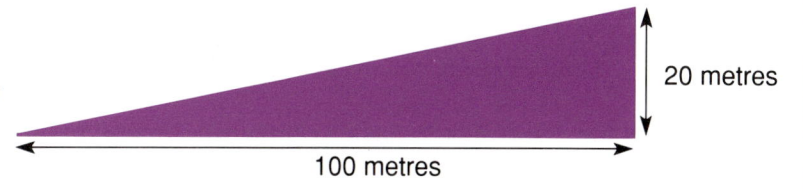

20 metres
100 metres

5 If you travel 100 metres horizontally how many metres would you rise vertically on these hills?

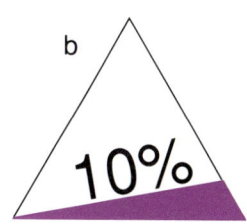

   a 25%   b 10%

These are the signs for the 3 hills on the German Course.

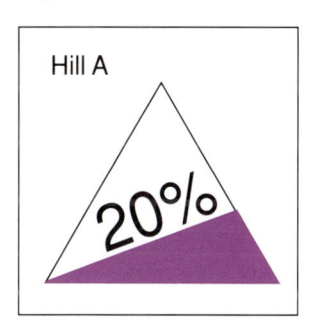

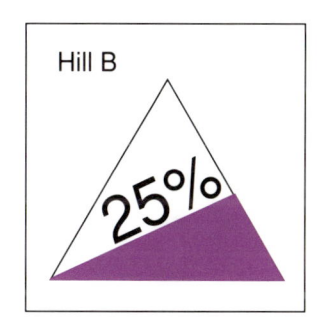

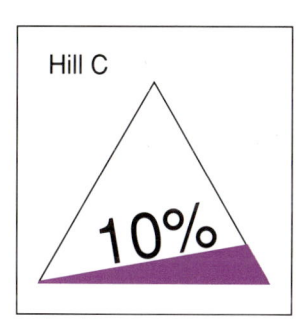

Hill A 20%   Hill B 25%   Hill C 10%

6 On Hill A how far do you travel horizontally if you rise:
   a 20 metres vertically?   b 10 metres vertically?
   c 5 metres vertically?   d 1 metre vertically?

7 Look at your table for the course in Wales.
   Which hill is steeper, Hill A in Wales, or Hill A in Germany?

8 Which hill in Wales has the same slope as Hill A in Germany?

9 Copy the unfinished signs below. Complete them using the German system.

   a 1:4 ↔   b 1:10 ↔   c 1:5 ↔

47

Connections

work with a friend

| Play Connections | A game for 2 players. |

Each player needs: A calculator, 13 counters of one colour.

Rules: Take it in turns to choose any 2 numbers from the 6 numbers in the **Connections List**.
You may add or subtract them.
Cover the answer on the grid with a counter.

The winner is the first player to have a chain of counters going from top to bottom or from side to side.

CONNECTIONS LIST
19, 26, 31, 43, 69, 114

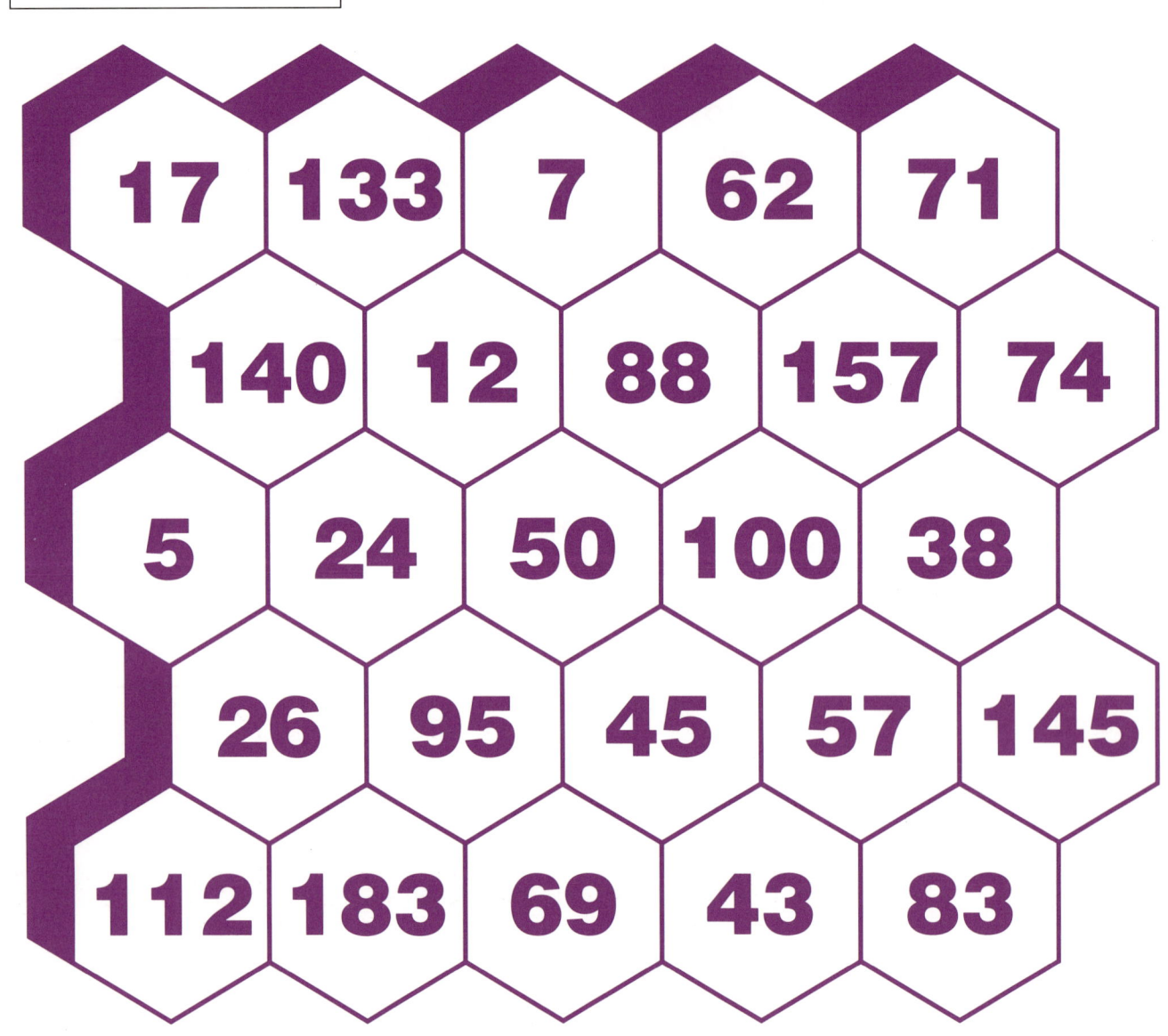

17 133 7 62 71
140 12 88 157 74
5 24 50 100 38
26 95 45 57 145
112 183 69 43 83

48

Connections

Play Super Connections

The rules are the same as before.
Use the **Super Connections List**.

This time you might not find your answer on the grid. If this happens you must wait until your next go for a chance to put a counter on the grid.

SUPER CONNECTIONS LIST
6, 29, 35, 58, 99, 105, 122, 169

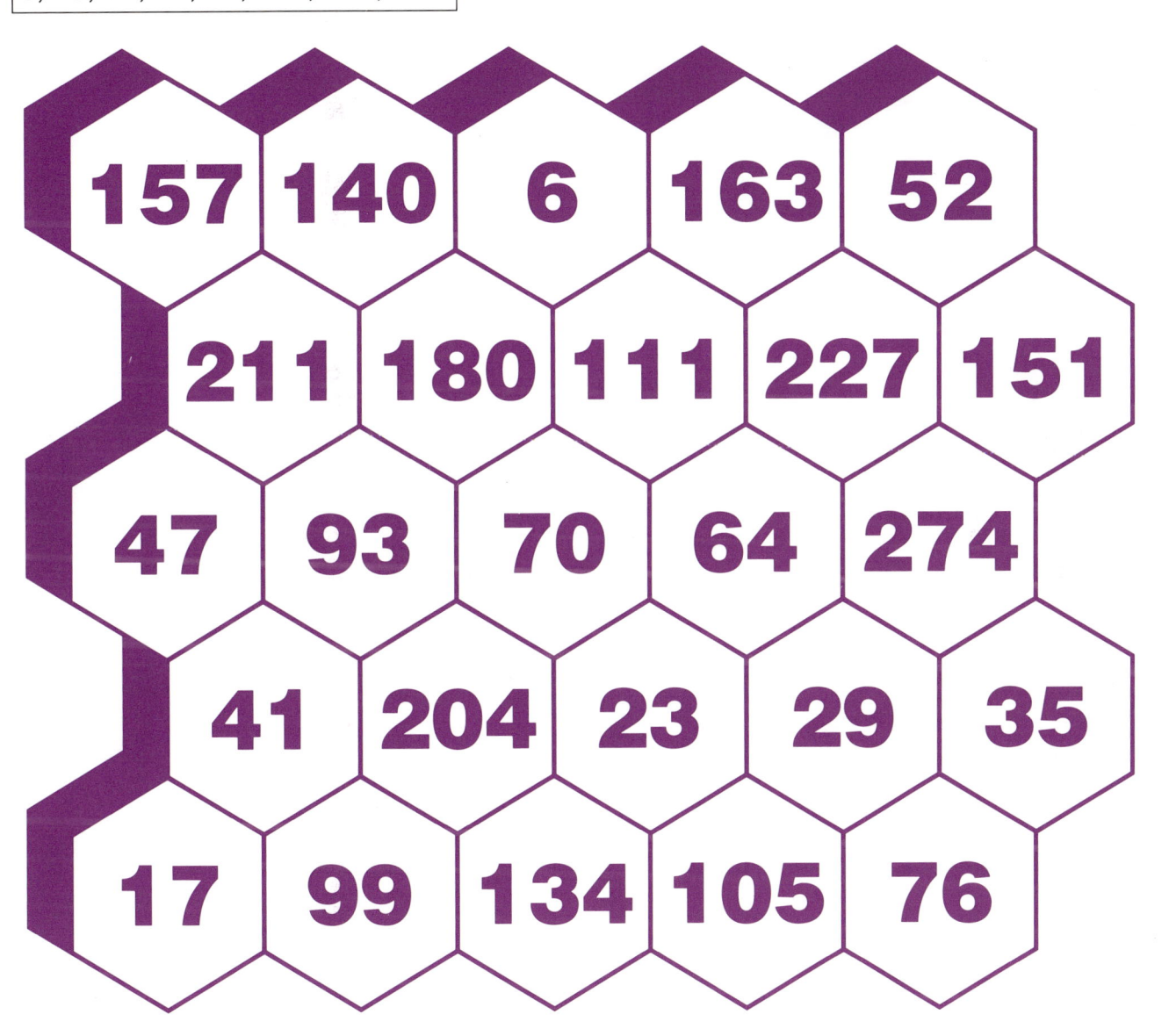

157	140	6	163	52
211	180	111	227	151
47	93	70	64	274
41	204	23	29	35
17	99	134	105	76

Growing up

This is part of the height chart of 2 sisters, Dionne and Joan.

2 y 9 m means 2 years 9 months

1. a How old was Dionne when her height was first recorded?
   b What was her height?

2. a How old was Joan when her height was first recorded?
   b What was her height?

3. How tall was Dionne when she was 3 years 3 months old?

4. How tall was Joan when she was 2 years 6 months old?

5. Copy this table
   Fill it in.

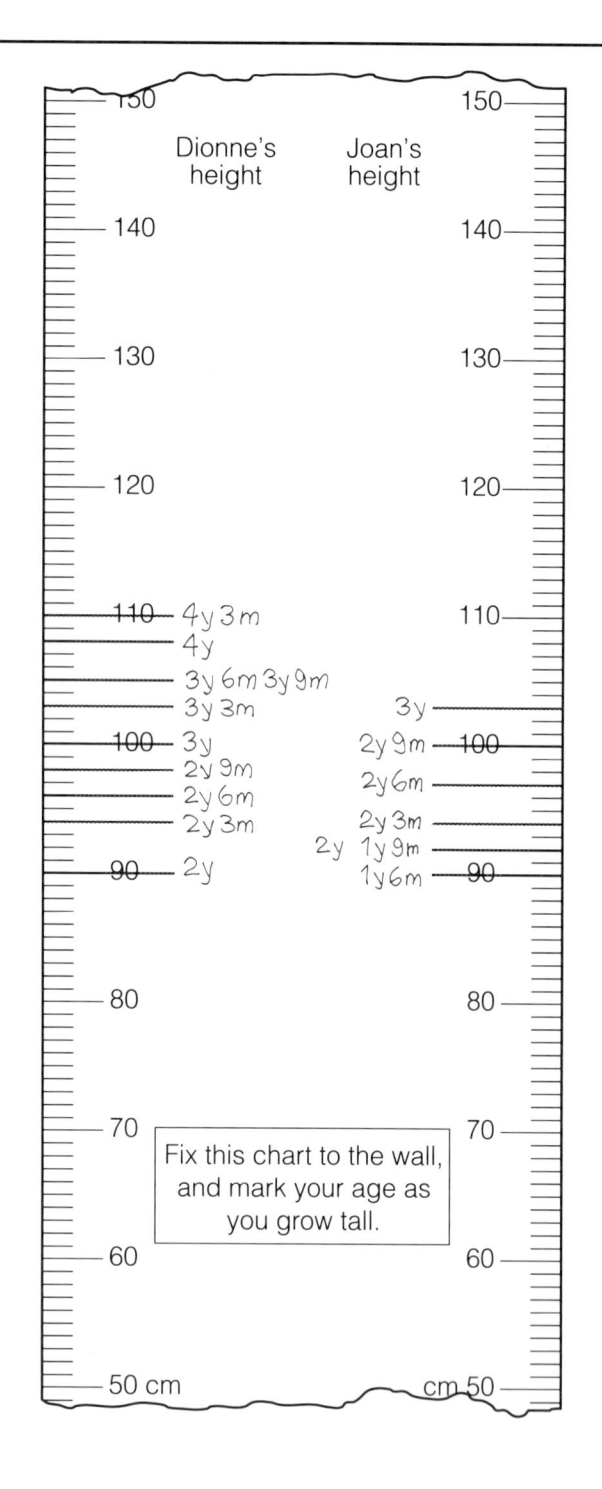

	1y 6m	1y 9m	2y	2y 3m	2y 6m	2y 9m	3y	3y 3m	3y 6m	3y 9m	4y	4y 3m
Dionne's height (cm)												
Joan's height (cm)												

Fix this chart to the wall, and mark your age as you grow tall.

Growing Up

6 Copy this graph. Use your table to help you to complete it for Dionne's height.

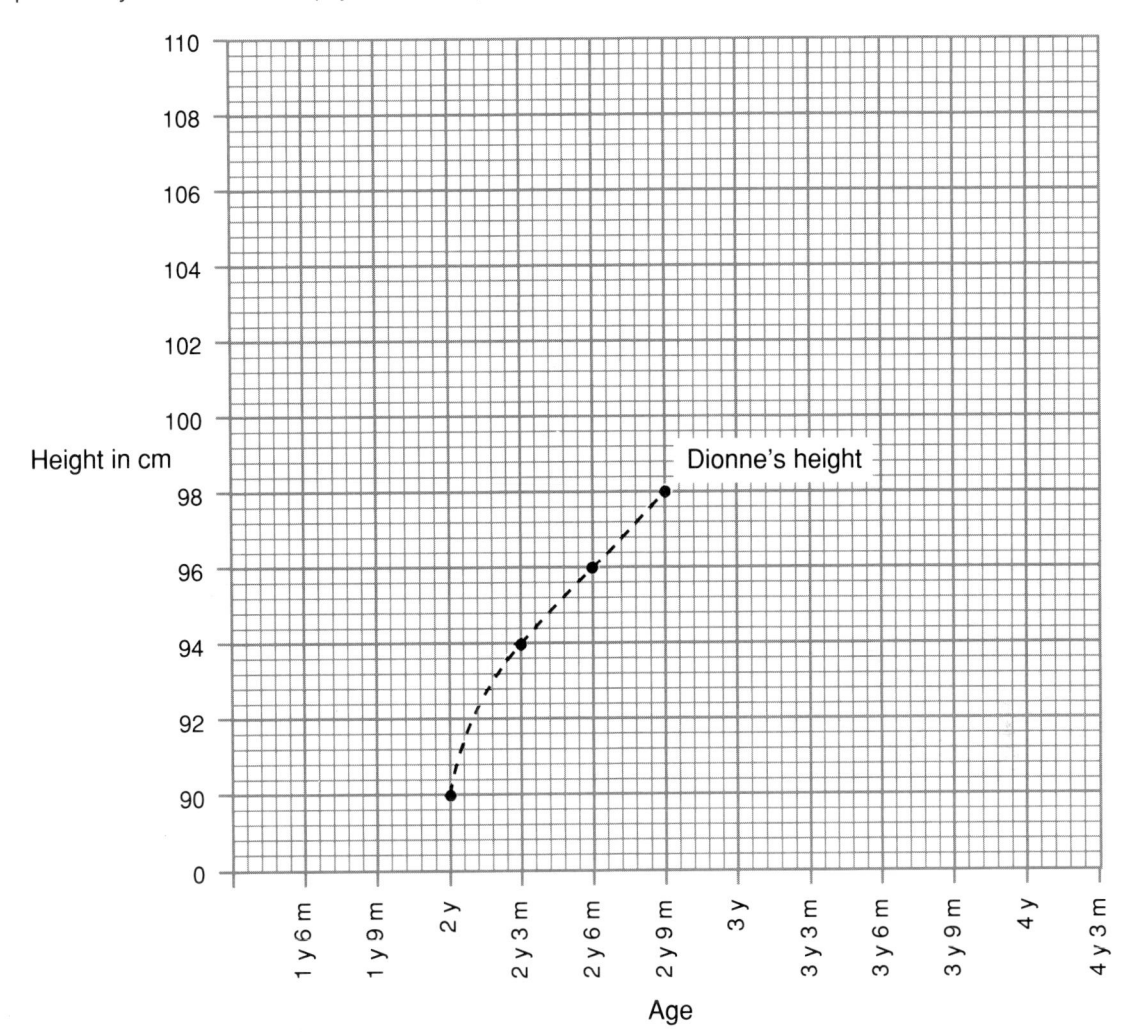

7 On the same graph mark Joan's height from 1 year 6 months to 3 years old.

Use your graph to answer these questions.

8 Who was the taller at 2 years old?

9 Dionne and Joan were the same height at the same age. What age was this?

10 a During which 3 months did Dionne's height stay the same?
   b What was her height?

11 a During which 3 months did Joan's height stay the same?
   b What was her height?

12 During which 3 months did Dionne grow most quickly?

The average height for a 3-year old is 98 cm.

13 Were Dionne and Joan above or below average height when they were 3 years old?

Electric Charge

Electricity is sold by the unit.

These are some of the things you can get for one unit.

Colour TV –
6 hours viewing

100 watt light –
10 hours lighting

Toaster –
70 slices

Cooker –
15 minutes cooking

3 kW heater –
20 minutes warmth

Kettle – water for
50 cups of tea

Stereo system –
10 hours music

60 watt light –
18 hours lighting

1 How many units are used up by:
   a a 3 kW heater in 1 hour?   b a colour TV in 3 hours?
   c a stereo system in 5 hours? d **two** 100 watt lights in 5 hours?

2 How many hours of cooking can you do:
   a for 4 units?   b for 8 units?

3 How many slices of toast can you make for 2 units?

4 How many cups of tea can you make for 3 units?

A unit of electricity costs 6.3p.

5 Work out to the nearest penny how much it costs:
   a to watch colour TV for 3 hours,   b to listen to a stereo for 5 hours,
   c to boil water for 25 cups of coffee, d to use a 3 kW heater for 3 hours,
   e to cook a turkey for 6 hours,   f to use five 100 watt lights for 10 hours.

Your answers to questions 1b and 1c will help you

Electric Charge

Sonia's flat has an electric slot meter.

She is having a party. This is what she thinks she will need.

6 List all the items. By the side of each one write down how many units of electricity are needed.

7 a How many units will Sonia use altogether?
   b How much will they cost?

8 Her slot meter only takes 10p pieces. How many will she need?

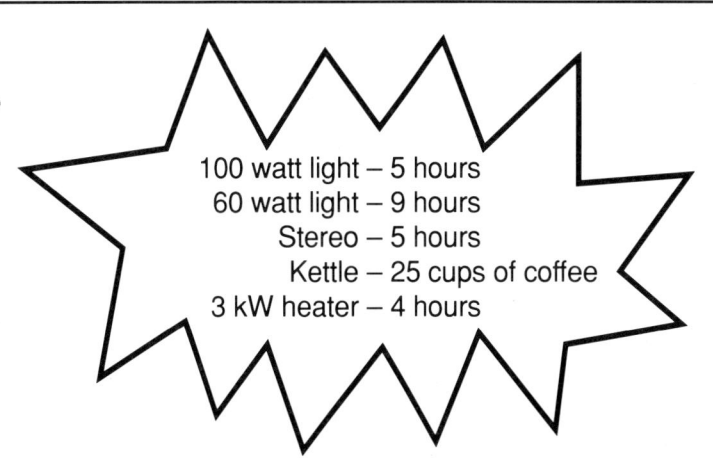

> 100 watt light – 5 hours
> 60 watt light – 9 hours
> Stereo – 5 hours
> Kettle – 25 cups of coffee
> 3 kW heater – 4 hours

Sonia's parents get an electricity bill like this every three months.

ELECTRICITY CHARGES FOR THE PERIOD ENDED   24 JUN 90

METER READING		UNITS USED	UNIT RATE (pence)	AMOUNT £	STANDING CHARGE £	VAT CODE	TOTALS £
PRESENT	PREVIOUS						
09081	08497	584	5.36	31.30	10.14	0	41.44

£ 41.44

9 Write down how you think the number of units in the 'UNITS USED' column is calculated.

10 Write down how you think the 'TOTALS' column is worked out.

11 During the whole of last year Sonia's parents used 5825 units of electricity. Work out the total amount they spent on electricity last year, at a unit rate of 5.36p.

Remember: There is a standing charge every three months

BUDGET PLAN

The electric company run a monthly budget payment plan. You pay a fixed amount each month, but first the company has to estimate your annual charges. This is how the budget plan works.

★ The company works out your annual cost based on the number of units you used last year.
★ An allowance is made for expected increases in charges.
★ The estimated annual bill is divided into equal monthly instalments.
★ The monthly payment is always a whole number of pounds.

12 How much do you think Sonia's parents' monthly payment should be?

Blocks and Cubes

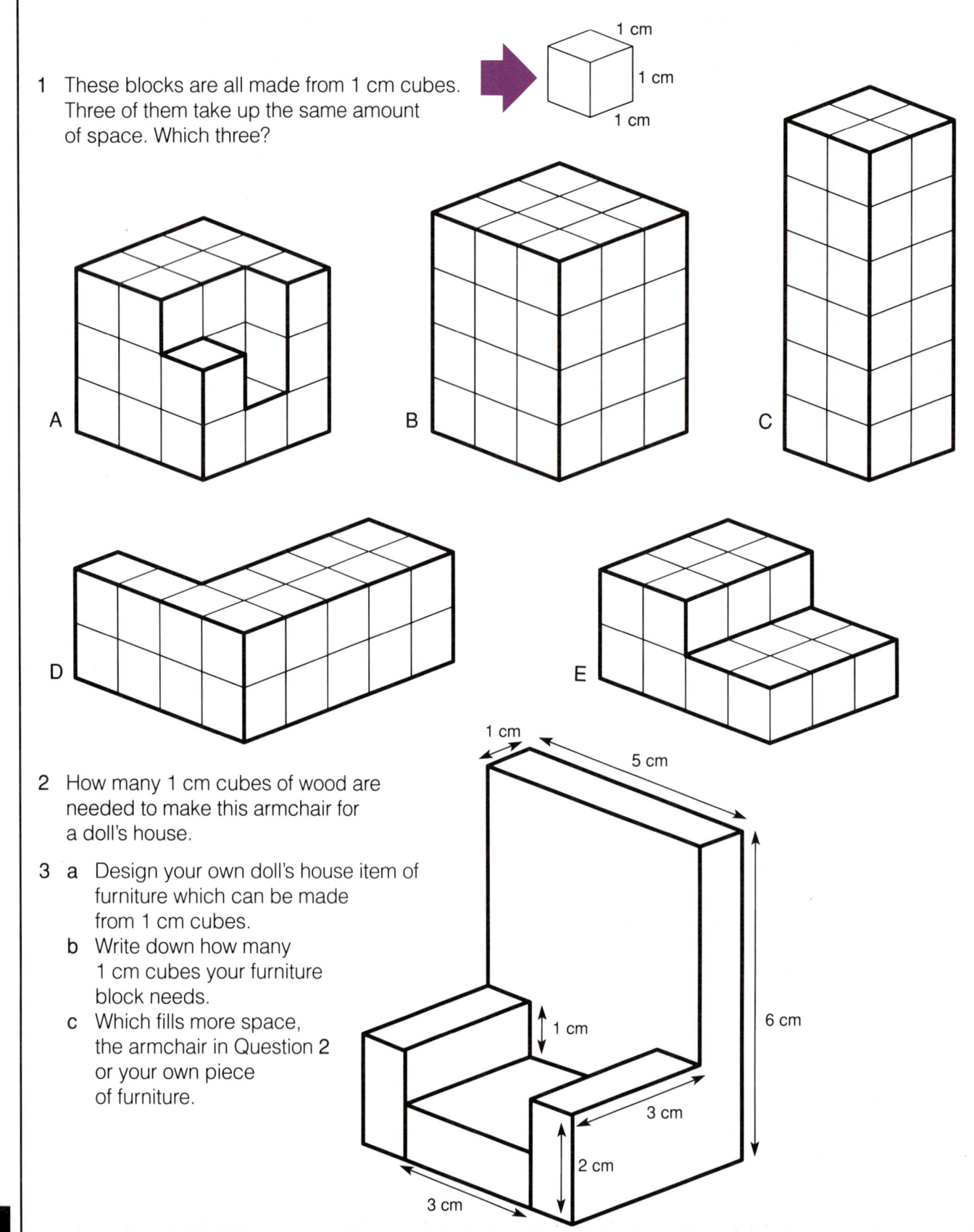

1. These blocks are all made from 1 cm cubes. Three of them take up the same amount of space. Which three?

2. How many 1 cm cubes of wood are needed to make this armchair for a doll's house.

3. a Design your own doll's house item of furniture which can be made from 1 cm cubes.
   b Write down how many 1 cm cubes your furniture block needs.
   c Which fills more space, the armchair in Question 2 or your own piece of furniture.

Blocks and Cubes

This block is made from eight 1 cm cubes. It takes up 8 cubic centimetres (8 cm³) of space. Its volume is 8 cm³.

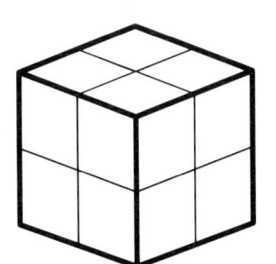

This block takes up 1cm³ less of space. Its volume is 7 cm³.

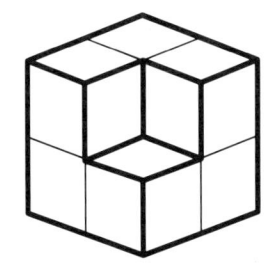

4 a What is the volume of each of the blocks in Question 1?
  b What is the volume of the armchair in Question 2?
  c What is the volume of your own piece of furniture in Question 3?

5 Imagine blocks **A** and **B** below cut into 1 cm cubes.
  a How many 1 cm cubes could you make from each block?
  b What is the volume of each block?

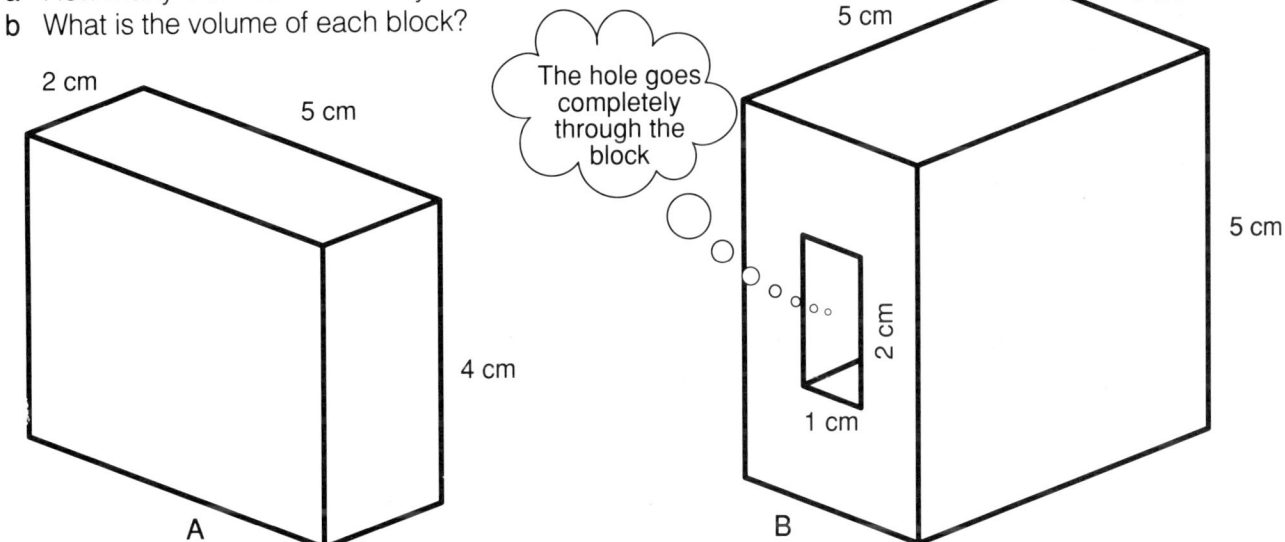

The hole goes completely through the block

VOLUME CHALLENGE

6 The drawings show how you can find the volume of the wedge. What is its volume?

7 a Find the volume of wedges A and B.
  b Sketch a wedge whose volume is 30 cm³.

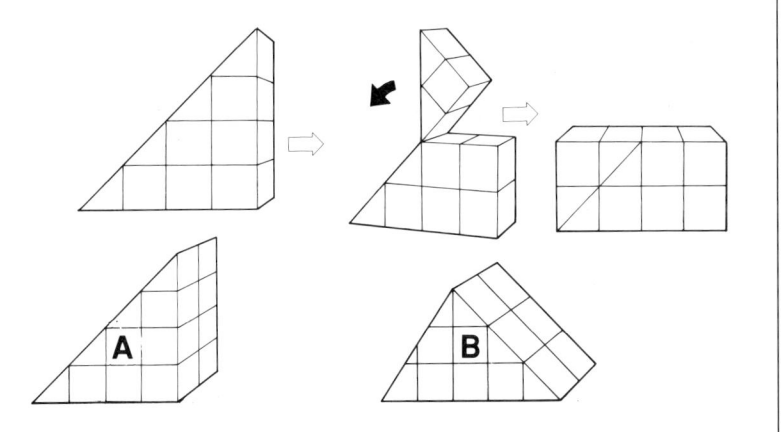

Crime News

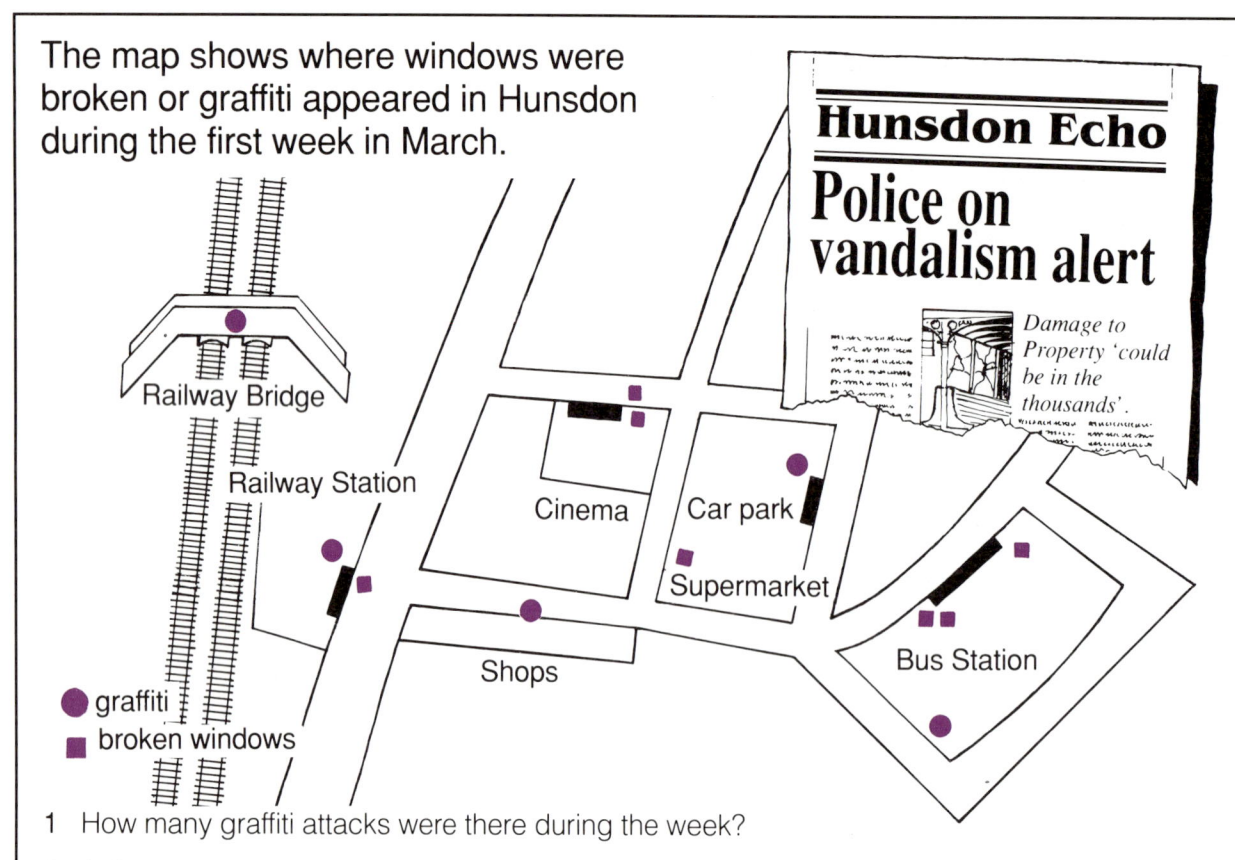

The map shows where windows were broken or graffiti appeared in Hunsdon during the first week in March.

Hunsdon Echo

Police on vandalism alert

Damage to Property 'could be in the thousands'.

● graffiti
■ broken windows

1. How many graffiti attacks were there during the week?
2. At how many sites were windows broken?
3. How many areas of damage were there altogether?

After 6 weeks the Hunsdon Echo printed this chart:

		Broken windows and graffiti attacks
March	Week 1	● ● ● ● ● ■ ■ ■ ■ ■ ■
	Week 2	● ● ● ● ■ ■ ■ ■ ■ ■ ■
	Week 3	● ● ● ● ● ■ ■ ■
	Week 4	● ● ● ● ■ ■ ■ ■ ■ ■
April	Week 5	● ■ ■ ■
	Week 6	

4. How many graffiti attacks were there altogether during the six weeks?
5. How many window breaking attacks were there?
6. In which week do you think the Echo printed this headline:

Vandalism: Police start special patrols.

Crime News

At the end of the year the Hunsdon Echo produced a special report on vandalism.

This chart went with the report:

7   In which month were there:
    a most attacks?
    b least attacks?

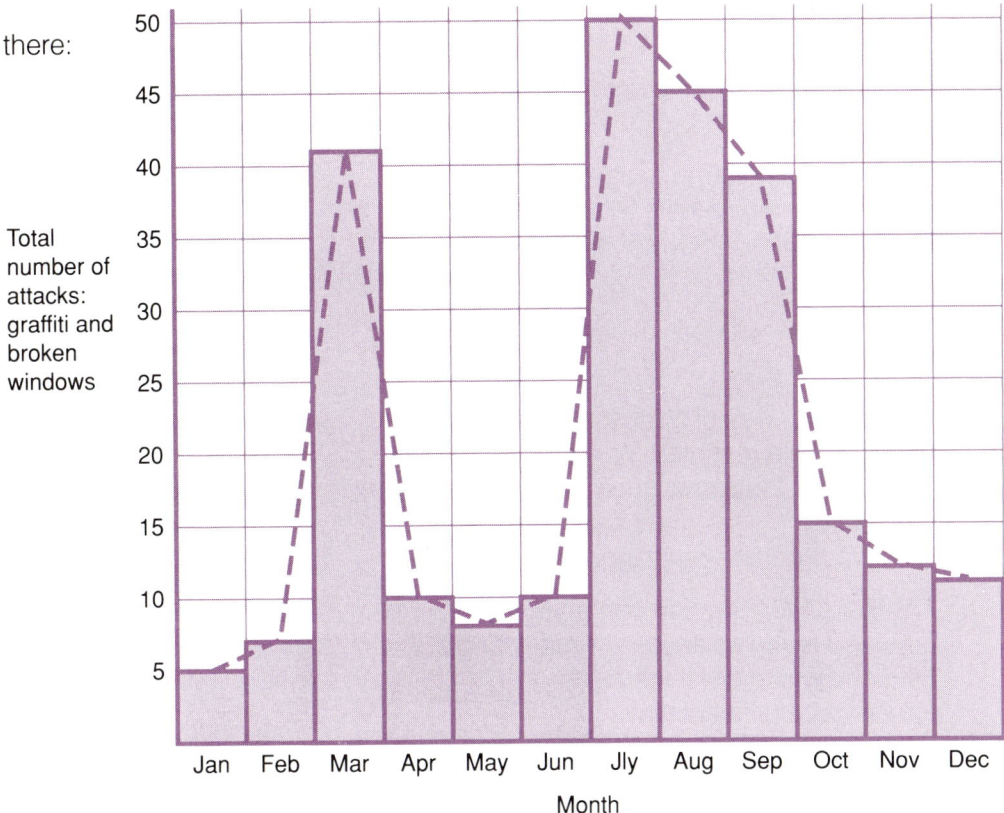

8   Copy this table. Use the graph to help you to complete it.

Month	Jan	Feb	Mar	Apr	May	June	July	Aug	Sept	Oct	Nov	Dec
Total number of attacks, graffiti and broken windows												

9   These are the figures for graffiti attacks each month.

Month	Jan	Feb	Mar	Apr	May	June	July	Aug	Sept	Oct	Nov	Dec
Graffiti Attacks	2	4	19	6	4	3	24	22	20	10	8	6

Use the table to help you to work out how many broken window attacks there were in:
    a February,   b July.

10 On the same grid draw two graphs like that at the top of the page.
    One graph should show the number of graffiti attacks.
    The other should show the number of broken window attacks.

11 Roughly, what fraction of all attacks involved:
    a graffiti?
    b broken windows?

57

Rotating Patterns

Here are four ways of putting together two red and two white triangles.

1. What special kinds of triangle have been used?
2. Copy each of the patterns onto triangular dotted paper.
3. a Which of the patterns can be folded to give a line of symmetry (mirror line)?
   b Draw in the lines of symmetry for each pattern.
4. Which pattern would look exactly the same if you gave it half a turn?
5. a Find another way of putting together two red and two white triangles. Your pattern must look exactly the same when you give it half a turn.
   b Draw your pattern on triangular dotted paper.
6. a Think of patterns which can be made from three red triangles and one white triangle. Find one which looks the same turned three different ways.
   b Draw your pattern on triangular dotted paper.

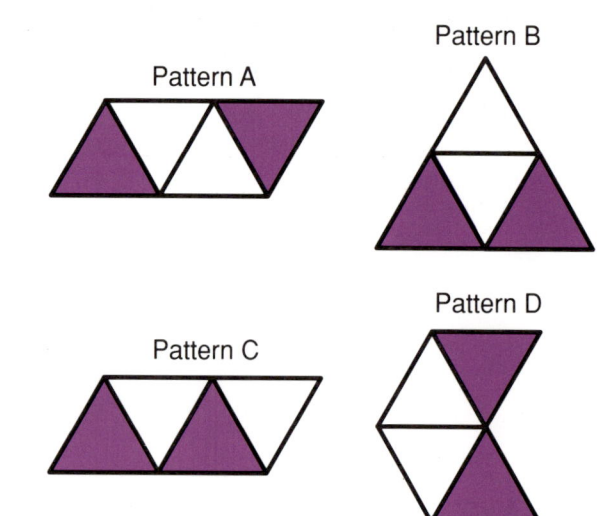

Here are four ways of putting together two red and two white squares.

7. a Which two patterns would look exactly the same if you gave them half a turn?
   b Draw them on square dotted paper.
8. Show how the squares in pattern A can be rearranged so that it looks exactly the same when you give it half a turn.

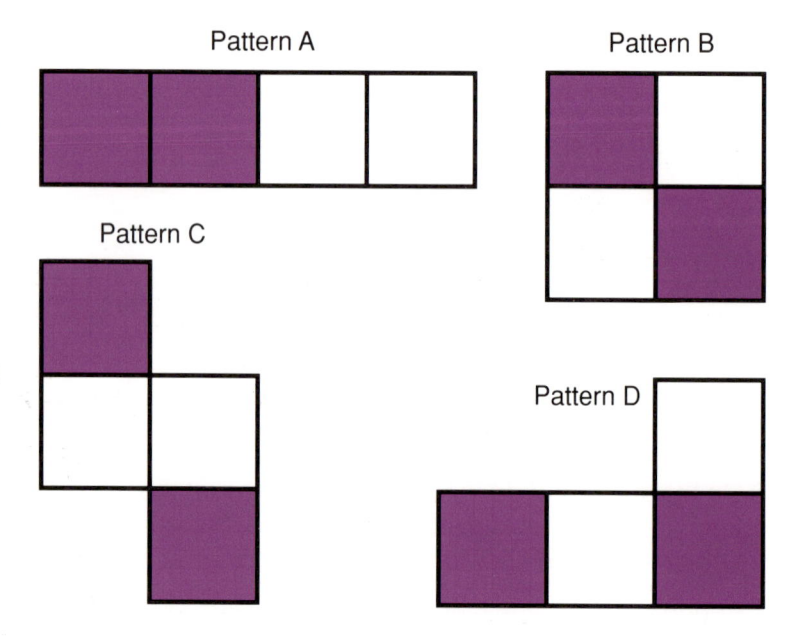

Rotating Patterns

A pattern that looks the same when turned around has **rotational symmetry**.
The number of different ways it can be turned to look the same is its **order of rotation**.

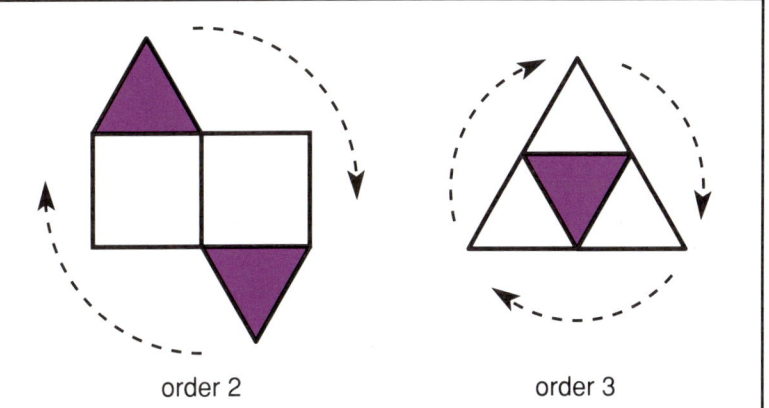

order 2   order 3

9 Write down the order of rotation for each of these patterns:

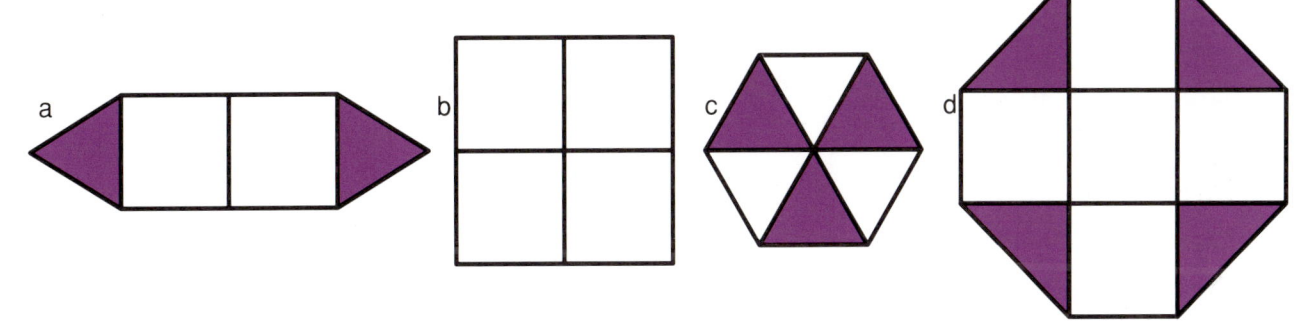

a   b   c   d

10 Draw patterns with order of rotation 2 which use:
   a three squares,
   b five squares,
   c six squares.
   Find as many different patterns as you can.

ROTATION IN USE

This car key fits into the lock in two different ways. The shape of the hole has order of rotation 2.

11 Find some more examples of how rotational symmetry is used at home or school. What order of rotation is used in each example?

infant toys

Fabric patterns

Going Home

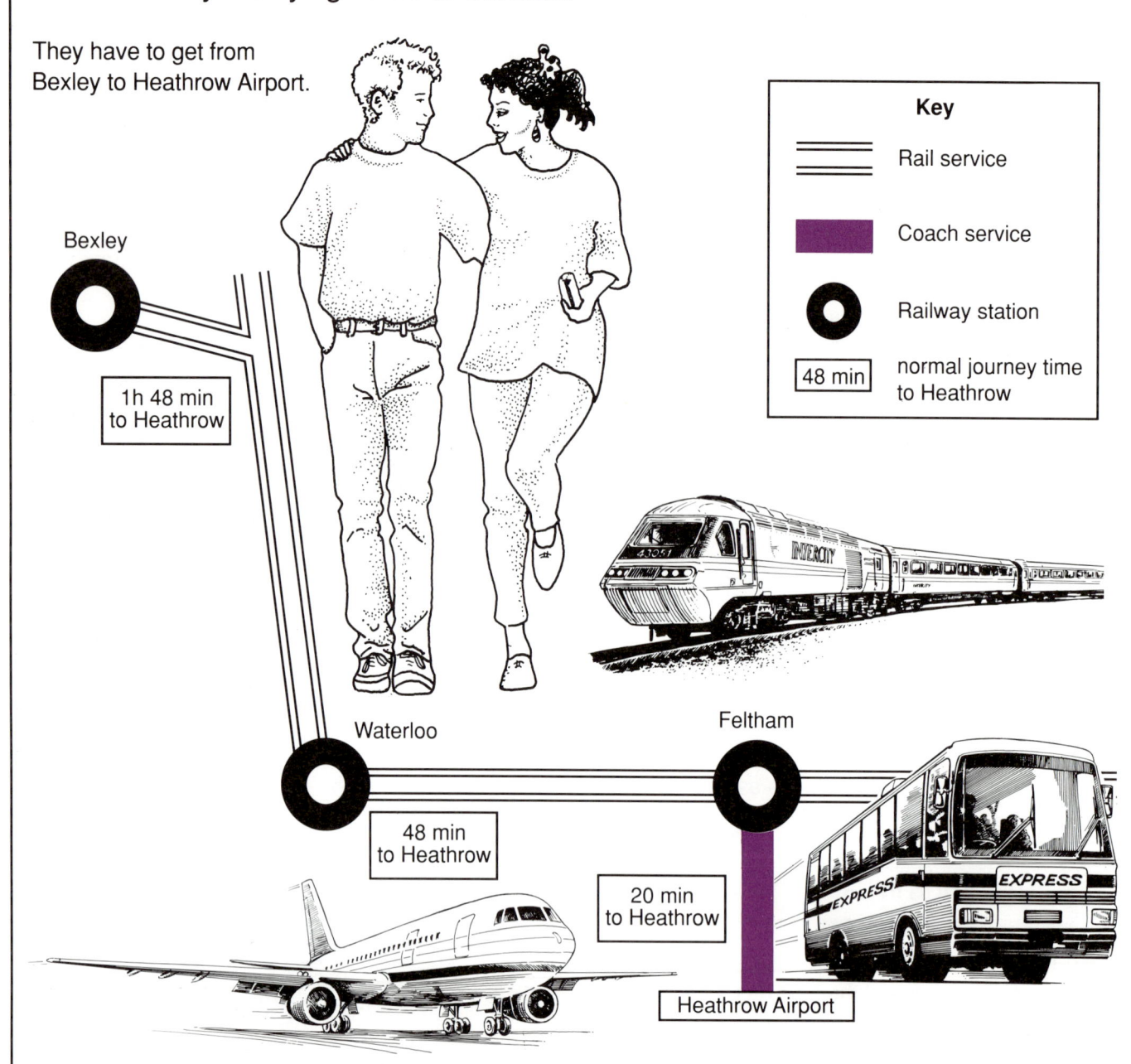

Tina and Gary are flying home to Canada.

They have to get from Bexley to Heathrow Airport.

Bexley

1h 48 min to Heathrow

Waterloo

Feltham

48 min to Heathrow

20 min to Heathrow

Heathrow Airport

Key

── Rail service

▇ Coach service

◉ Railway station

48 min — normal journey time to Heathrow

1. What part of Gary's and Tina's journey is by train?
2. What part of their journey is by coach?
3. What is the normal journey time to Heathrow:
   a from Feltham?
   b from Waterloo?
4. Work out the normal journey time from Bexley to Waterloo.

Going Home

Passengers from Bexley must change trains at Waterloo.

The timetables give train and coach times between Waterloo and Heathrow.

5 a What time does the 09.22 train from Waterloo arrive in Feltham?
   b What time does the connecting coach leave Feltham?
   c What time does this coach arrive in Heathrow?

6 What time does the next train, after the 09.22:
   a leave Waterloo?
   b arrive in Feltham?

Train		Coach	
Weekdays		Weekdays	
Waterloo Depart	Feltham Arrive	Feltham Depart	Heathrow Arrive
06.52	07.17	07.20	07.40
07.11	07.38	07.50	08.10
07.52	08.14	08.20	08.40
08.22	08.44	08.50	09.10
08.52	09.14	09.20	09.40
09.22	09.44	09.50	10.10
then every half hour until		then every half hour until	
16.52	17.15	17.20	17.40
17.12a	17.38	17.50	18.10
17.22b	17.44	17.50	18.10
17.52a	18.15	18.20	18.40
17.52b	18.14	18.20	18.50
18.22	18.44	18.50	19.10
18.52	19.14	19.20	19.40
then every half hour until		then every half hour until	
20.52	21.14	21.20	21.40
21.22	21.44	21.50	22.10

Tina's and Gary's plane takes off at 13.20.
They must check in at the airport one hour before take-off.

7 What time must they check in?

This is the part of the timetable they need to plan their journey.

8 Copy the timetable. Fill it in.

Train		Coach	
Waterloo Depart	Feltham Arrive	Feltham Depart	Heathrow Arrive
09.22	09.44	09.50	10.10
09.52	10.14	10.20	
10.22			
		11.20	
		11.50	
11.52			

9 What is the last coach they can catch from Feltham to check in on time?

10 Which train should they catch from Waterloo to connect with this coach?

11 Work out the latest time Tina and Gary can catch a train from Bexley so that they can check in on time. (Your answer to question 4 will help you).

61

Mind that Child!

Claire's parents left some pills where she could reach them. Claire was lucky – the doctors saved her life.

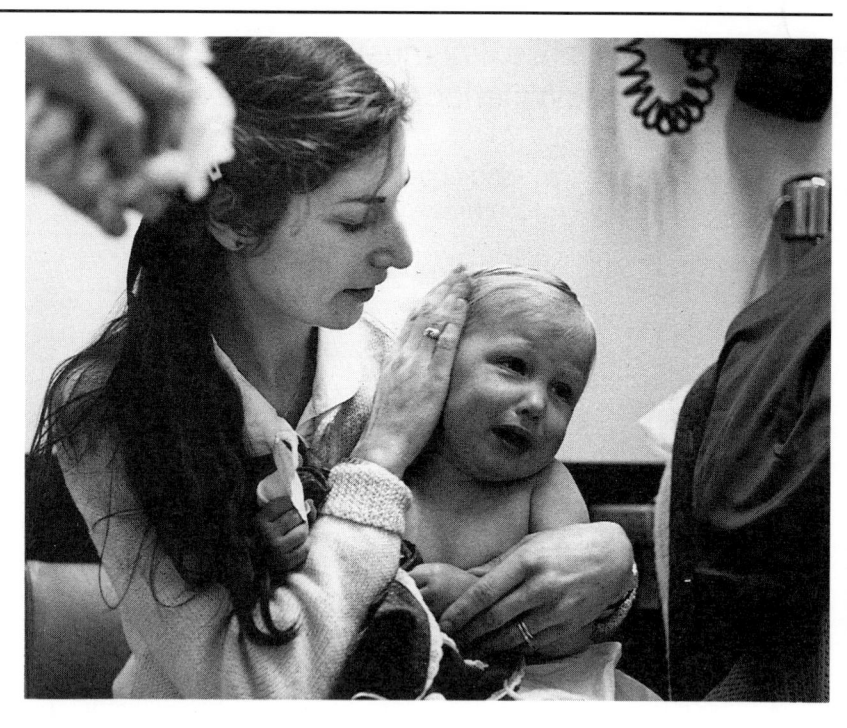

This bar chart shows the number of children in Claire's town who were admitted to hospital due to poisoning.

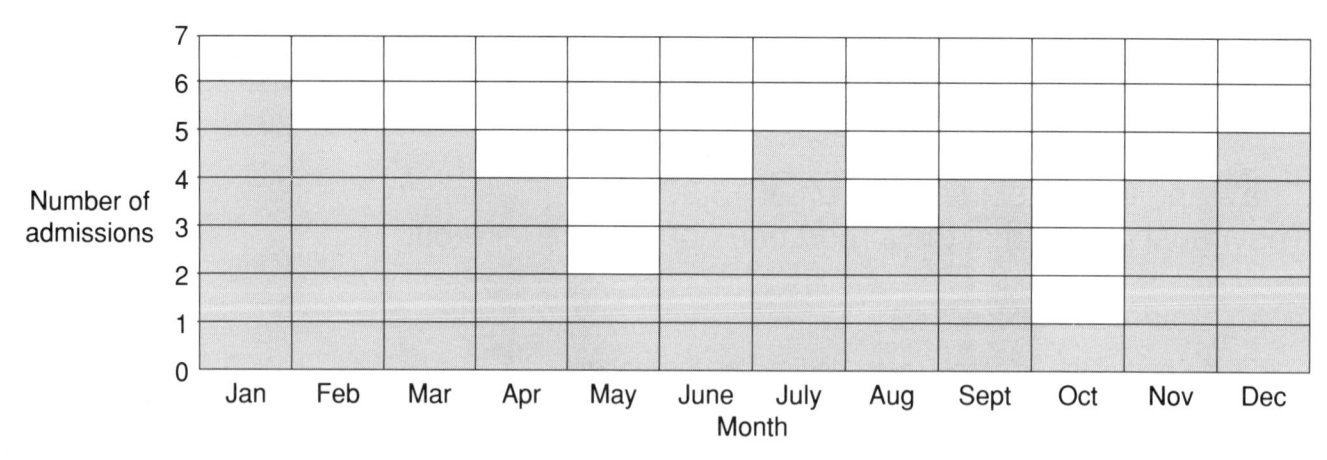

1 How many children were admitted to hospital:
   a in January?
   b in May?
   c in October?

2 During which month were:
   a the greatest number of children admitted?
   b the least number of children admitted?

3 How many children were admitted:
   a during the first half of the year?
   b during the whole year?

4 On average, how many children were admitted each month?

Mind that Child!

Claire was just one of many children in her town admitted to hospital after an accident in the home.

This graph shows the number of hospital admissions for the main types of accident in the home.

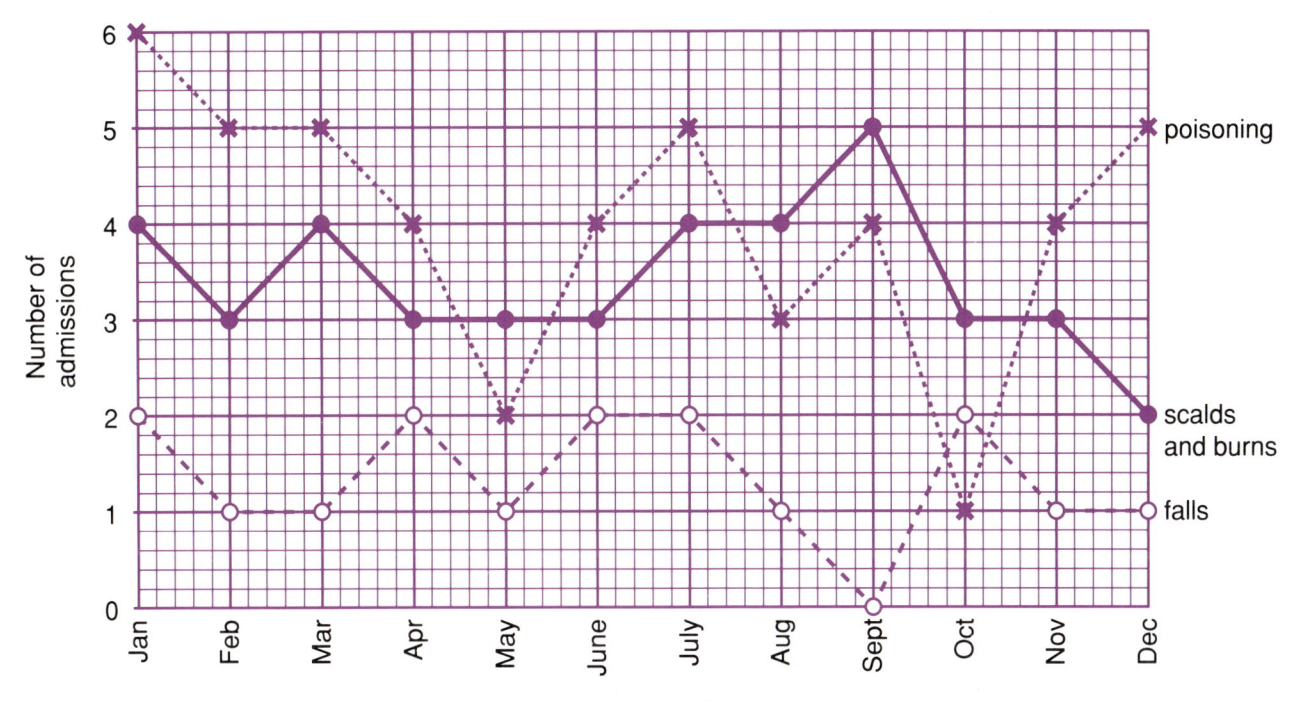

5 What three types of accidents are shown on the graph?

6 How many children were admitted to hospital in July suffering from:
   a poisoning?
   b scalds and burns?
   c falls?

7 Copy this table. Use the graph to help you fill it in.

| Accident | Number of children admitted to hospital in: |||||||||||| Total |
	Jan	Feb	Mar	Apr	May	June	July	Aug	Sept	Oct	Nov	Dec	
Poisoning	6	5	5										
Scalds and burns	4	3											
Falls	2												
Total	12												

8 Which was the most common type of accident?

9 How many children altogether were admitted to hospital after an accident in the home?

10 Design a poster warning parents of the dangers to children in the home.
   Show how many children are seriously hurt.

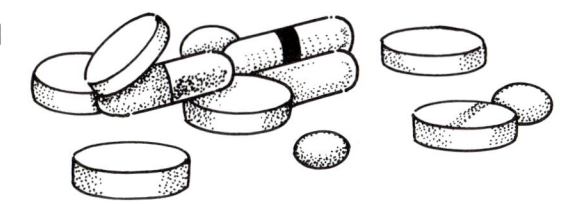

Parcel Post

Neera works in the Post Room at Khan Electronics.

She weighs the parcels and puts stamps on them ready for posting.
Here are 5 different parcels she must weigh.

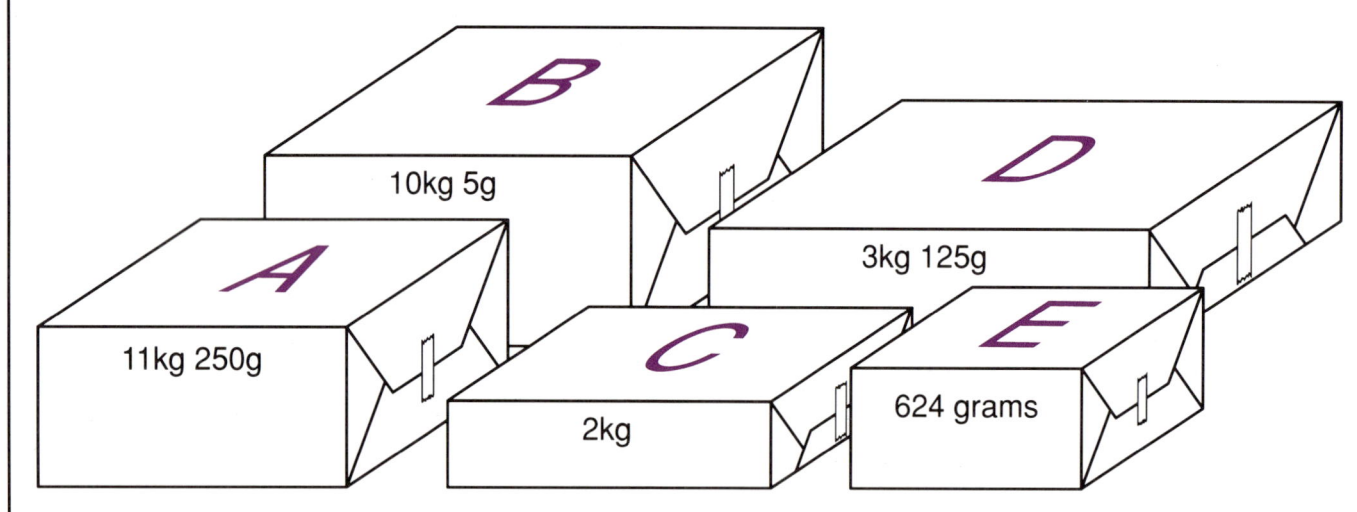

- A: 11kg 250g
- B: 10kg 5g
- C: 2kg
- D: 3kg 125g
- E: 624 grams

1. Which parcel is:
   a the heaviest?
   b the lightest?

2. Which parcels weigh more than 3 kg?

3. Which parcel weighs more than 3 kg but less than 4 kg?

4. Which parcel is not over 1 kg in weight?

To decide the postal costs Neera uses this table:

From 5th September
This tariff applies to parcels posted and delivered within the U.K.

PARCEL POST

Weight not over		Weight not over	
1 kg	£1.70	7 kg	£3.45
2 kg	£2.10	8 kg	£3.60
3 kg	£2.60	9 kg	£3.85
4 kg	£2.80	10 kg	£4.00
5 kg	£3.00	25 kg	£5.00
6 kg	£3.30		

5. How much will it cost to post a parcel of 6 kg or less?

6. How much will it cost to post a parcel weighing between 8 kg and 9 kg?

7. How much will it cost to post:
   a parcel D?
   b parcel C?

8. Which two parcels will cost the same amount to post?

9. What is the heaviest parcel you can post for £4.00?

Parcel Post

Khan Electronics make electronic instruments.
One of the timers weighs 550 grams with its packing.

10 How much do 2 timers with their packing weigh:
   a in grams?
   b in kilograms and grams?

11 How much will it cost to post:
   a 1 timer?
   b 2 timers in one parcel?

Neera decides she needs a table like this:

Number of timers per parcel	1	2	3	4	5	6	7	8	9	10
Weight	550g	1Kg 100g	1Kg 650g	2Kg 200g						
Postage	£1.70	£2.10	£2.10							

12 Copy and complete the table.

The firm wants to insure parcels whose contents are worth £150 or more.
These are the insurance rates:
Each timer is worth £25.

13 How much are 6 timers worth?

14 How much will it cost to insure 6 timers?

15 What is the least number of timers the firm will insure?

ROYAL MAIL PARCELS
INSURANCE

By paying the fee you can insure your parcel against loss or damage in transit.

Compensation up to	Fee (in addition to postage)
£70	35p
£130	45p
£230	65p
£360	80p

16 Copy and complete this list:

Number of Timers	Total value	Cost of insurance
6	£150	65p
7	£175	
8		
9		
10		

Neera sends a parcel containing 10 electronic timers by post.

17 How much does it cost altogether including postage and insurance?

Fuel Savers

In the Rover Economy Trial each car has to travel as far as it can on 1 litre of petrol.

Each car has three runs.
The table shows their results.

Rover Car models	Number of kilometres travelled on 1 litre of petrol		
	1st run	2nd run	3rd run
Mini City	17.0	16.8	16.9
Metro City X	16.4	16.7	17.0
MG Maestro 2.0i	12.5	12.7	12.3
Montego 2.06Si	12.6	12.3	12.3
Rover 820E	11.9	11.3	11.3

1 Which car travelled furthest on its first run?

2 How far did the Mini travel **altogether** on its 3 runs?

3 How many litres of petrol did the Mini use **altogether**?

4 What was the average distance the Mini travelled on 1 litre of petrol?

5 For each of the other cars, work out the average distance it travelled on 1 litre of petrol.

6 Which of the five cars is most economical?

Jeffrey has bought a new car. These are his journeys for a week.

Day	Mon	Tues	Wed	Thur	Fri	Sat	Sun
Distance travelled (km)	35	35	49	102	63	106	142
Petrol brought (ℓ)	10		8	10	9	8	

7 How far did he travel during the week?

8 How much petrol did he buy?

9 How far did he travel on average per litre of petrol?

10 Which car do you think Jeffrey bought?
    Write down a reason for your answer.

Fuel Savers

Here are the results for makes of cars entered for the Small Cars Class.

11 List the cars. By the side of each write down:
   a the total distance travelled in 3 runs,
   b the average distance travelled on 1 litre of petrol.

12 Which of these cars is most economical?

Small models	Number of kilometres travelled on 1 litre of petrol		
	1st run	2nd run	3rd run
Mini City	17.0	16.8	16.9
Suzuki Alto	17.6	17.9	18.5
Peugeot 205XE	16.4	16.1	16.7
Citroen BX17RD	16.3	16.3	16.6
Ford Escort 1.4L	14.8	14.7	15.2
Nissan Micra SL	17.0	17.0	16.7
Ford Fiesta	17.2	17.3	18.0
Renault 4TC	16.1	15.2	15.8
Peugeot 309XL	14.8	15.0	15.2
Volkswagon Polo	17.1	16.9	17.0
Vauxhall Astra Merit	15.0	15.3	15.3

PETROL OR DIESEL

13 Look at the newspaper article. Use the information below to decide whether the claim in the report is true.

Diesel models	Number of kilometres travelled on 1 litre of petrol		
	1st run	2nd run	3rd run
Citroen BX17RD	17.1	17.1	17.4
Peugeot 309XLD	17.2	16.9	17.8
Vauxhall Astra DL	17.3	17.4	17.2
Escort DL	18.1	18.3	18.5

★ **Daily News** ★

Save money with diesel

Motorists can get an extra 2 kilometres on average from every litre of fuel if they drive diesels, a new report claims.

1. Follow the **flow chart**.
   Check that it gives this **sequence** of numbers:

   2, 5, 8, 11, 14, …

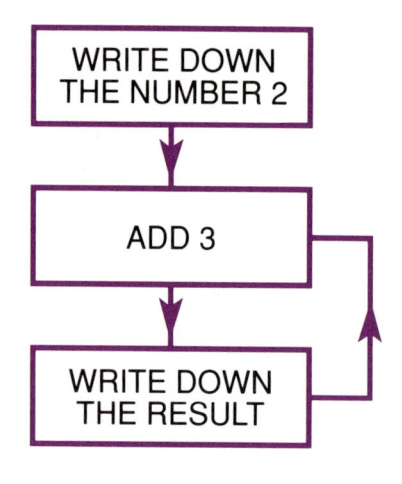

2. Change the instruction
      'Add 3'
    to 'Add 5'
   Write down the first five numbers
   in the new sequence.

3. The flow chart was changed again
   for this sequence:

   2, 12, 22, 32, 42, …

   Draw the new flow chart.

4. Draw a flow chart which gives this sequence:

   7, 14, 21, 28, 35, …

5. Draw a flow chart which gives this sequence:

   30, 27, 24, 21, 18, ……..

6. An instruction is missing from this flow chart.
   Find the missing instruction for each of these sequences:

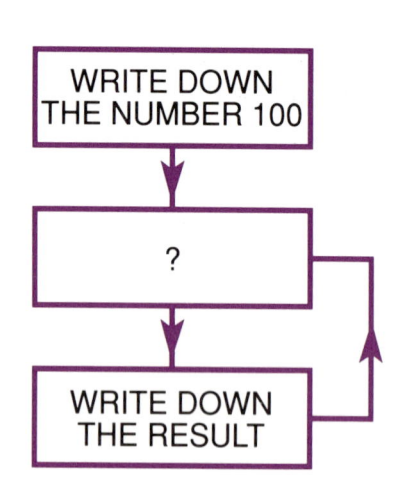

   a
   100, 105, 110, 115, …

   b
   100, 90, 80, 70, …

   c
   100, 87, 74, 61, …

   d
   100, 300, 500, 700, 900, …

   e
   100, 200, 400, 800, 1600, …

7 Follow the flow chart.
  Check that it gives this sequence of numbers:

  # 34, 16, 36, 36, 36, ...

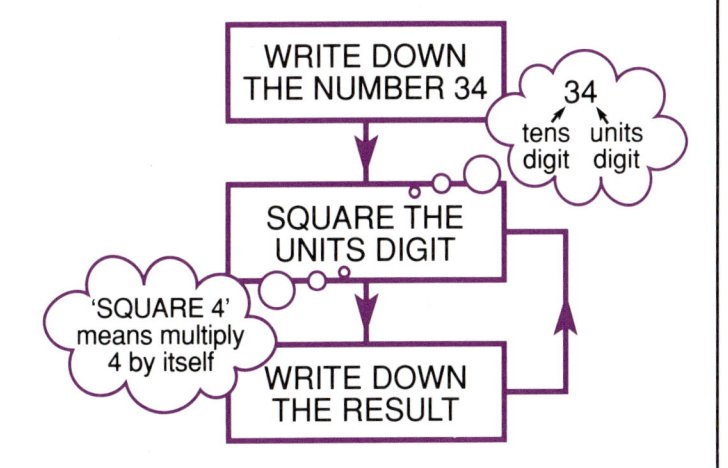

  WRITE DOWN THE NUMBER 34

  34 — tens digit, units digit

  SQUARE THE UNITS DIGIT

  'SQUARE 4' means multiply 4 by itself

  WRITE DOWN THE RESULT

  We can also show what the flow chart gives like this, as an arrow chart:
  Once we get to 36, we 'loop' to 36 for ever and ever.

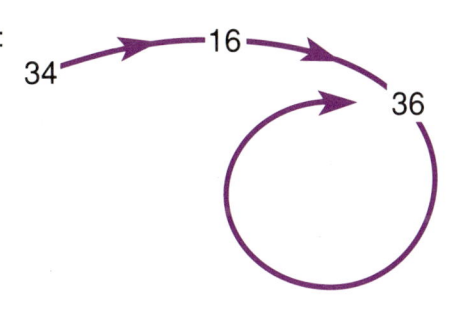

  34 → 16 → 36 (loop)

8 Start with the number 27.
  a Write down the sequence the flow chart gives.
  b Draw an arrow chart for the sequence.

LOOP NUMBERS

Numbers which loop to themselves are called 'loop numbers'.

For example, 36 is a 'loop number'.
In question 8 you will have found that 1 is a 'loop number'.

9 Find all the possible 'loop' numbers'.

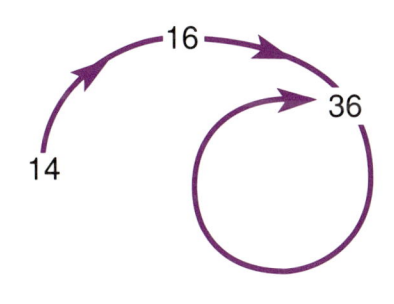

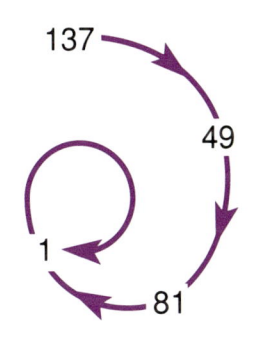

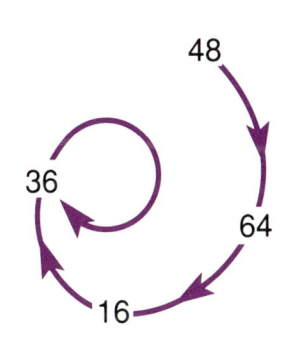

14 → 16 → 36 (loop)

137 → 49 → 81 → 1 (loop)

48 → 64 → 16 → 36 (loop)

U-Boat Attack

You are a radar operator on the HMS Dolphin.

At 06.00 the radar screen looks like this.

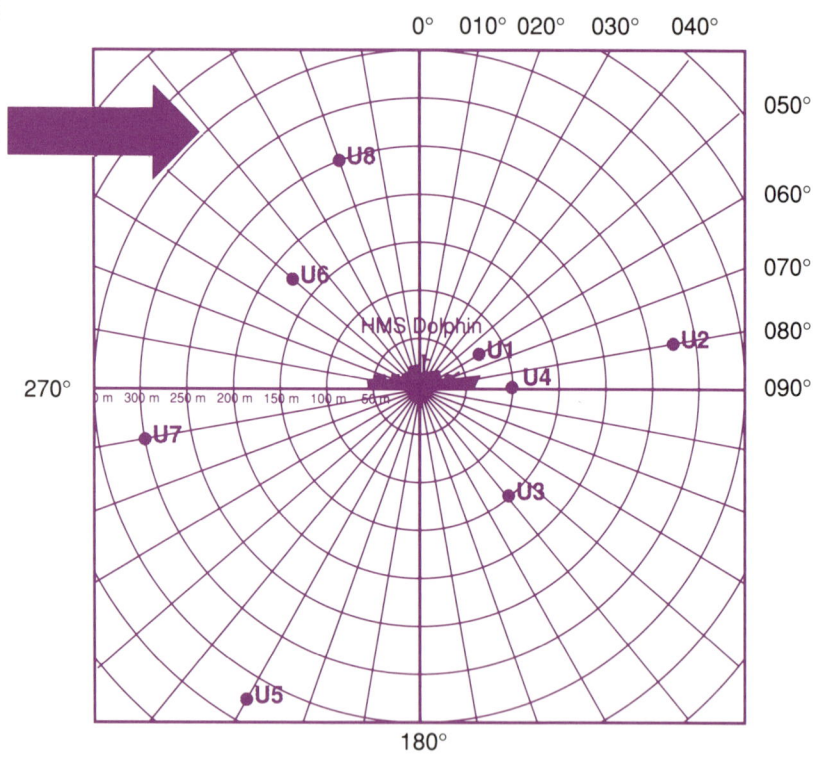

Your ship is surrounded by U-boats.
Find U-boat U1 on the radar screen. It is on the bearing 060° from HMS Dolphin.

1. Your Captain asks for the direction of each U-boat. List the U-boats.
   Write down the direction of each from HMS Dolphin like this: U1 060°
   U2 080°

2. On the radar screen U5 is furthest from the ship. Which U-boat is nearest?

3. List the U-boats in order of distance from the ship, nearest first.
   Write them down like this: U1 ➡ U4 ➡ ...

U-Boat Attack

The circles on the radar screen are 50 metres apart.
So U3 is 150 metres from HMS Dolphin at 06.00.

4 How far away from the ship is U4 at 06.00?

The depth charge range from HMS Dolphin is 200 metres.

5 Which U-boats are within firing distance at 06.00?

At 06.15 the radar screen looks like this.

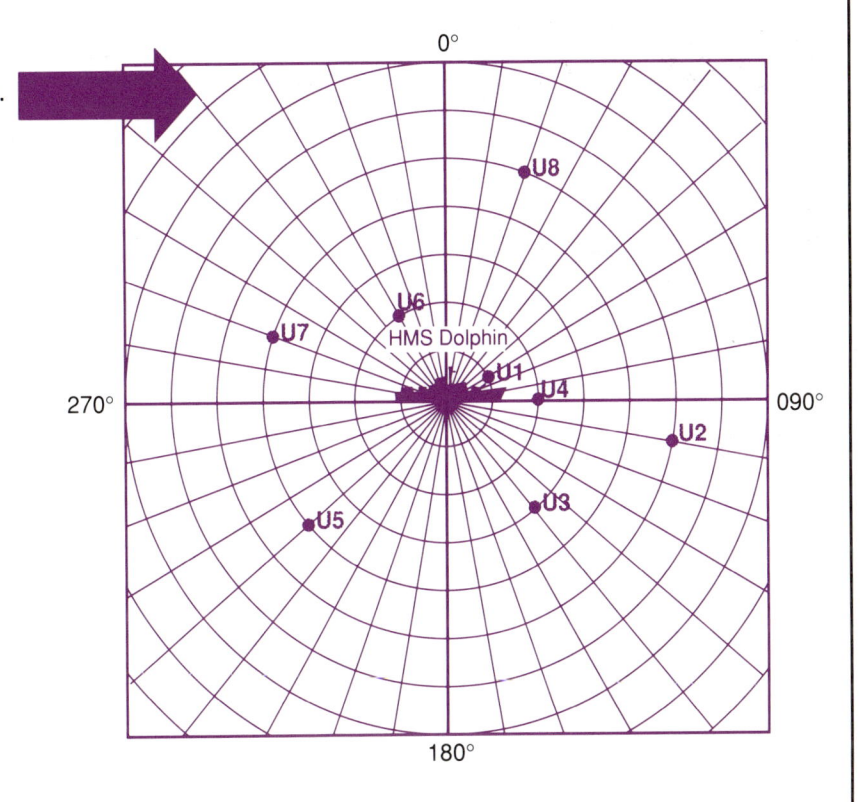

6 Copy this table.
   Fill in the direction and distance from
   HMS Dolphin of each U-boat.

U-Boat	Direction	Distance
U1	060°	50 m
U2		
U3		
U4		
U5		
U6		
U7		
U8		

7 Two U-boats have not moved.
   They were hit by depth charges at 06.00.
   Which ones were they?

8 Which other U-boats are within depth charge
   range at 06.15?

On the road

Joe and Bill are drivers for *Marsden's Cold-Store* firm. They have to transport meat from Springton to Skepton.

The map shows the Springton and Skepton depots.

Springton Depot

Springton
Penge
B404
B313
B149
Bridge Load Limit 28 tonnes
Elsden
River Stermy
East Ling
B717
Bridge Load Limit 20 tonnes
B404
B313
Banner
B149
Bridge Height Limit 4.0 m
Langton
Stanton
B149
Manston
B404
Axton
B149
Bridge Load Limit 32 tonnes
Bridge Height Limit 3.9 m
B404
Ling
B5194
Brierly
Hindleigh
Paxton
Bridge Load Limit 25 tonnes
B404
Croftley
Bridge Height Limit 4.0 m
Bridge Height Limit 4.4 m
Railway
Narrow Bridge 2.2 m
B313
Berndale Brook
River Stermy
Fenwick
Barley
B9057
Stoneleigh
Dronhill
B149
Skepton

Skepton Depot

72

On the Road

1 Springton is on the B 313. Find Manston.
  Which road is this village on?

2 Write down which villages are on the B 404.

3 Find Stoneleigh. Which road is it on?

4 How wide is the bridge near Stoneleigh?

5 How many railway bridges are marked with
  heights on the map?

6 How many road bridges over the River Stermy
  are marked on the map?

7 What is the tonnage of the heaviest transporter
  that can cross the River Stermy?

8 What is the height of the tallest transporter that
  can pass under **all** the railway bridges?

9 What is the height of the tallest transporter that can get from Springton to Skepton on the B 313?

10 What is the tonnage of the heaviest transporter that can get from Springton to Skepton on the B 313?

> Joe drives a 30-tonner (fully loaded).
> It is 3.9 m high and 2.4 m wide.

11 Work out the route Joe has to take to get from Springton to Skepton.
   Write down all the villages he has to pass through.

> Bill drives a 22-tonner (fully loaded).
> It is 4.1 m high and 2.15 m wide.

12 Work out the route Bill has to take to get from Springton to Skepton.
   Write down all the villages he has to pass through.

Folding Triangles

You need: a supply of A4 scrap paper
scissors
protractor
squared paper

1 a Fold a sheet of A4 paper along one diagonal. Cut along the fold line.
   b Measure the angles of one of the shapes you have made. Write their size on the shape.
   c Each shape is a special kind of triangle. Write down what you think is special about it.

2 Using one of your right angled triangles make a fold through one of its corners to make two smaller right angled triangles.

3 Use another sheet of A4 paper.
   a With **one fold** and one cut make a square.
   b Make a sketch of your square.
   c On your sketch mark in the fold line.
   d The fold you made divides the square into two special triangles. Write down what you think is special about them.

4 a The photograph shows a door wedge. One of its faces is a right-angled triangle. Sketch the triangle and mark the right angle with a "⌐".
   b Write down two more everyday things which have a right-angled triangle in them.
   c Measure and draw one of your triangles using squared paper. (You may need to draw it to scale).

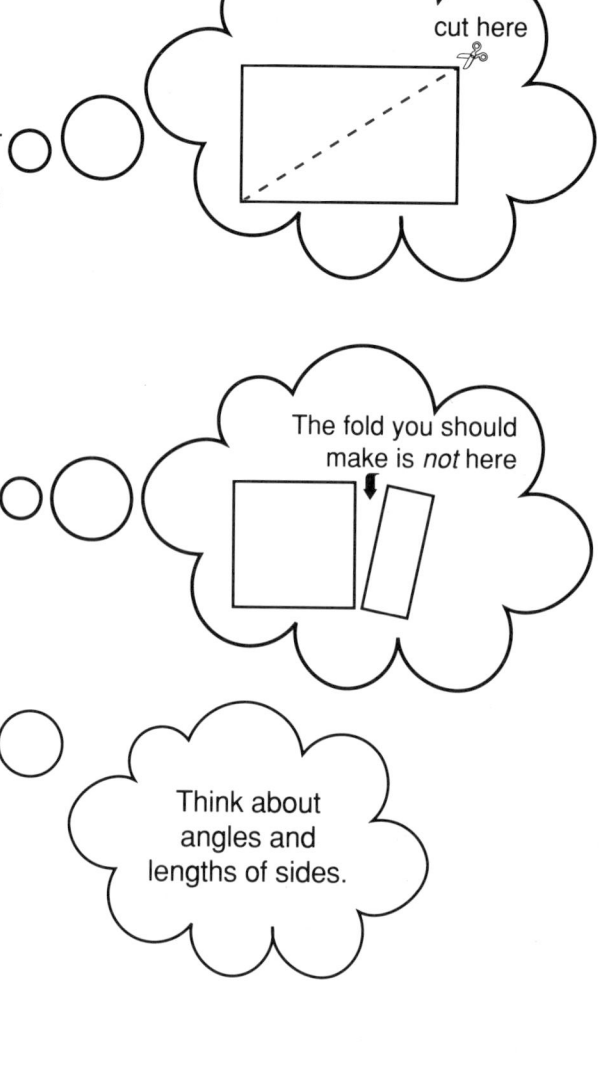

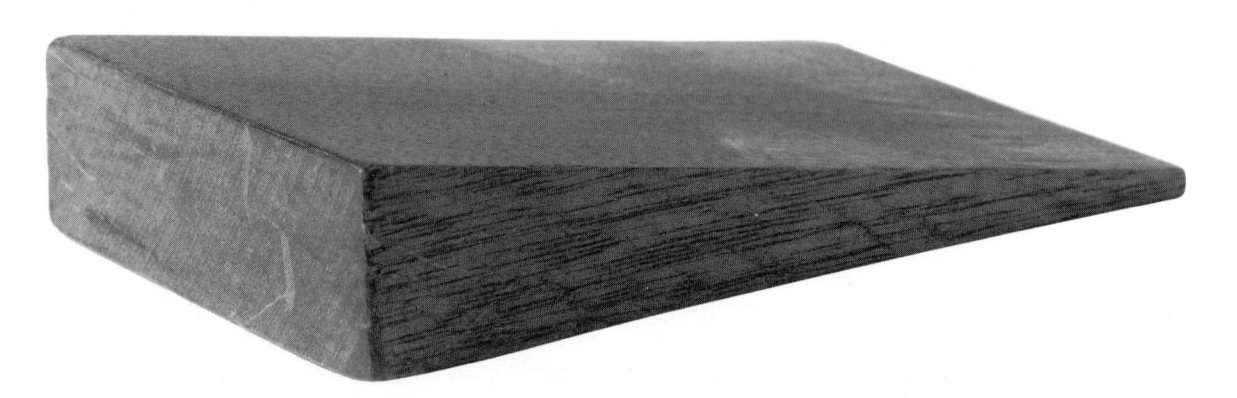

cut here

The fold you should make is not here

Think about angles and lengths of sides.

Folding Triangles

5 Fold another A4 sheet of paper in half, like this.
   a With one cut make a triangle which has two equal sides and two equal angles.
   b Measure the lengths of the sides and sizes of the angles. Mark them on your triangle.

6 The triangle you have just made is an **isosceles triangle**. There is an isosceles triangle in this photograph of a pair of stepladders.
   Sketch it and mark the equal angles and equal sides.

7 a Write down two more everyday things which have an isosceles triangle in them.
   b Measure and draw one of your triangles. (You may need to draw it to scale).

EQUILATERAL TRIANGLES

An equilateral triangle has all three sides and all three angles equal.

work with a friend

8 a Each of you fold an equilateral triangle from an A4 sheet of paper like this:

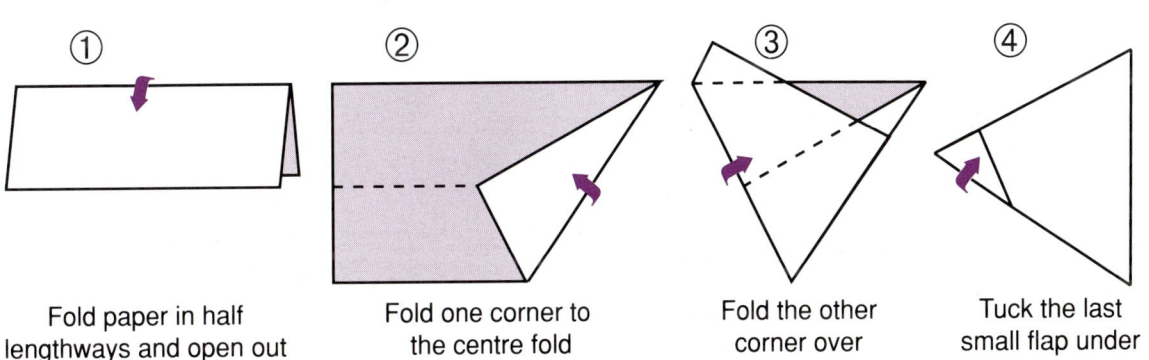

① Fold paper in half lengthways and open out

② Fold one corner to the centre fold

③ Fold the other corner over

④ Tuck the last small flap under

   b Measure the angles of your triangle. What size is each one?
   c Make more equilateral triangles so that you have six altogether. Draw all the different shapes you can make by fitting them together.

75

Check it out

These are the exact prices and some rough estimates for the boots, tennis racket and shirt.

£28.70
About £30

£16.45
About £15

£8.99
About £10

Do questions **1–3** in your head.

1. Check that the boots and tennis racket cost about £45.

2. Find the approximate cost of:
   a. the boots and the shirt,
   b. the tennis racket and the shirt,
   c. all three items.

3. These are three attempts to find the total cost of the items using a calculator: Which do you think is most likely to be correct?

   541.4   54.14   135.05

4. Use your calculator to find the exact cost of the three items. Was your answer to Question 3 correct?

Number Fashion.

5. These are the attendance figures for the three days of a fashion show:
   Monday 765   Tuesday 986   Wednesday 824
   About 750   About......   About......

   a. Write down your own approximations for Tuesday's and Wednesday's figures.
   b. These are three attempts to find the total attendance for Monday, Tuesday and Wednesday using a calculator. Which do you think is most likely to be correct?

   2575   22475   1985

   c. Use your calculator to check your choice in **b**.

Check it out

6 a The bath robes were about £30 before the sale. In the sale they are about £25. About how much do you save?
   b Use your calculator to work out exactly how much you save.

Bath robes

Sale
were £32.45
Now only £24.75

7 a The car cost about £4500 before the sale. Write down a rough estimate for its price in the sale.
   b In your head decide which of these is most nearly correct for how much you save:
      i £1000   ii £600   iii £1600
   c Use your calculator to work out exactly how much you actually save.

was £4475
Now only £3854

8 These numbers tell you how many flights there were from an airport in four different weeks.
   a Write down your own approximations for the numbers of flights.

Week 1	Week 2	Week 3	Week 4
4176	2986	805	1448
About 4000	About...	About...	About...

   b Use your list of approximations to decide which of these statements are likely to be correct.
   i   7162 aeroplanes flew from the airport in weeks 1 and 2.
   ii   3253 aeroplanes flew from the airport in weeks 3 and 4.
   iii 44340 aeroplanes flew from the airport in weeks 2 and 4.
   iv   643 more aeroplanes flew from the airport in week 4 than in week 3.
   v   1190 more aeroplanes flew from the airport in week 1 than in week 2.
   vi   1581 more aeroplanes flew from the airport in week 2 than in week 3.

CALCULATORS WHICH GET IT WRONG

9 a **In your head** work out 10 ÷ 3 × 3.
   b On your calculator press

   [C] [1] [0] [÷] [3] [×] [3] [=]

   Does your calculator give 10 or 9.999999999?
   c Which is the correct result, 10 or 9.999999999?
   d Try to explain why some calculators give the 'wrong' answer.
   e Find another example where a calculator sometimes gives the 'wrong' answer. Use a different dividing number to 3.

THINK:
If I divide by 3 then multiply by 3, what happens?

Display stands

One of the display stands used in the shop window looks like this:

It is made by cutting each face (side) from a sheet of plywood.

1. How many pieces must be cut from a sheet of plywood to make the stand?

2. How many of these pieces are:
   a rectangles?
   b triangles?

3. Make a sketch of one of each kind of piece needed. Mark the measurements of the sides on each sketch.

4. a Use card or squared paper. Make a scale drawing of the five pieces needed to make the stand.
   b Cut the pieces out. Stick them together with sellotape to make a model of the display stand.

Use a scale of 1 cm for each 10 cm

A model of the display stand can also be made from this **single** piece of card.
This is called a **net** of the stand.

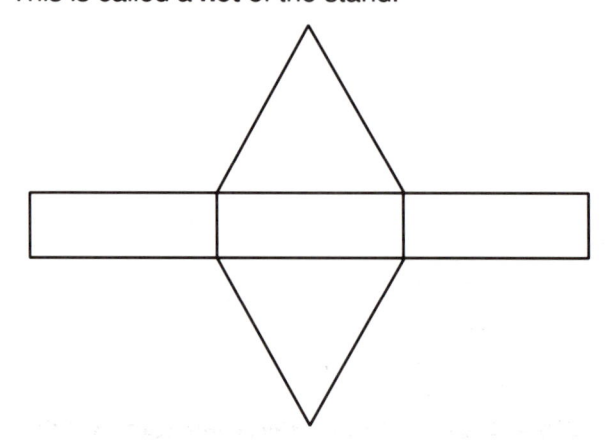

5. Sketch the net from which you can make this display stand.

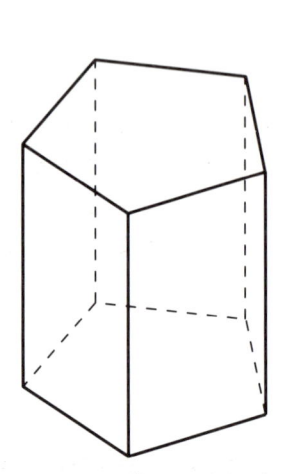

Display Stands

Here are some different display stands.

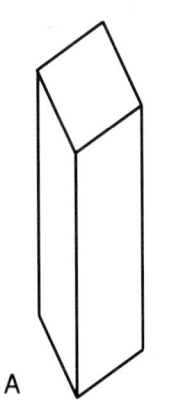

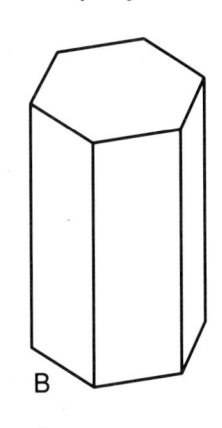

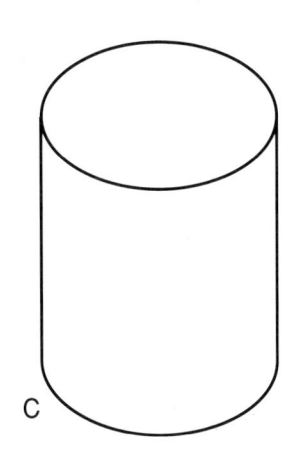

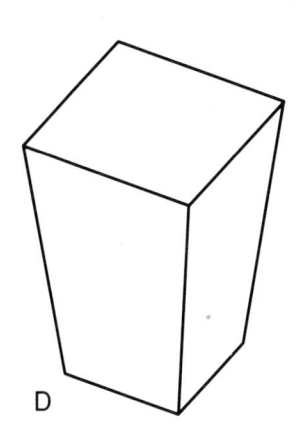

A B C D

These are the nets for making them.

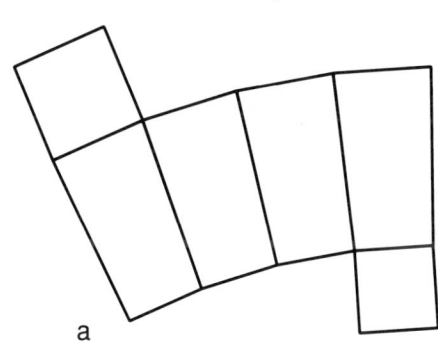

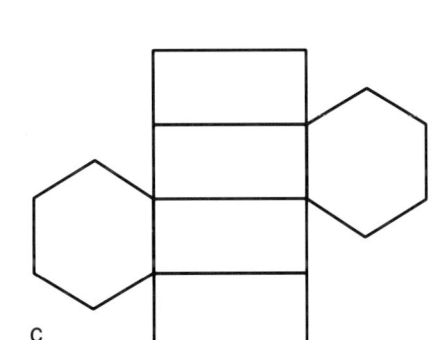

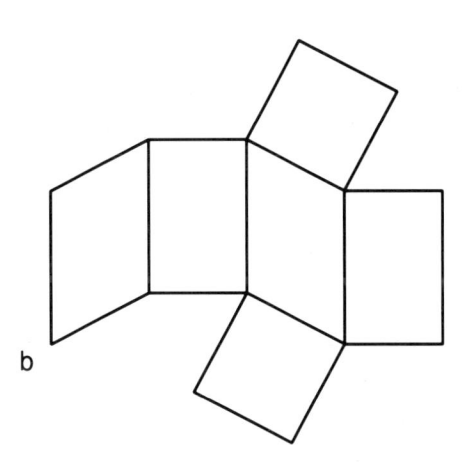

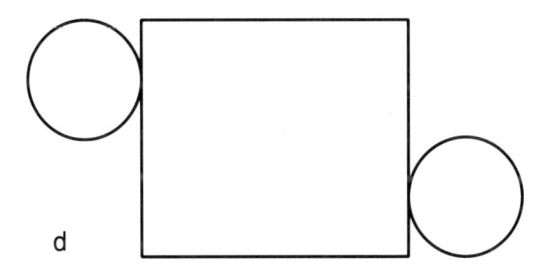

a b

c d

6 Match each net with a display stand. Write your answers like this: A↔? B↔? etc.

YOUR OWN DESIGN

7 a Design your own display stand for this trophy.
   b Make a scale drawing of its net.
   c Make a paper or card model of your stand.

Dominoes

This is a DOUBLE 2 set of dominoes.

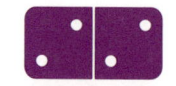

1. How many dominoes are there in the set?
2. What is the highest double?

Double one.... Double two....?

This is a DOUBLE 3 set.

3. What is the highest double?
4. How many dominoes are there in this set?
5. How many more are there in this set than a DOUBLE 2 set?

There are five more dominoes in a DOUBLE 4 set than in a DOUBLE 3 set. Here are three of them.

6. Draw the other two.
7. How many dominoes are there altogether in a DOUBLE 4 set?
8. Copy this table. Complete it for a DOUBLE 4 set.

	DOUBLE 1 set	DOUBLE 2 set	DOUBLE 3 set	DOUBLE 4 set	DOUBLE 5 set	DOUBLE 6 set
Number of extra dominoes		3	4			
Total number in the set	3	6	10			

9. Complete the table for a DOUBLE 5 and DOUBLE 6 set.
10. How many dominoes are there in:
    a. a DOUBLE 7 set?
    b. a DOUBLE 9 set?
    c. a DOUBLE 12 set?

Work with a partner						Dominoes

You will need scissors and card.

Matching Chains

Work together to make a DOUBLE 3 set of dominoes out of card.

Each domino should look like this:

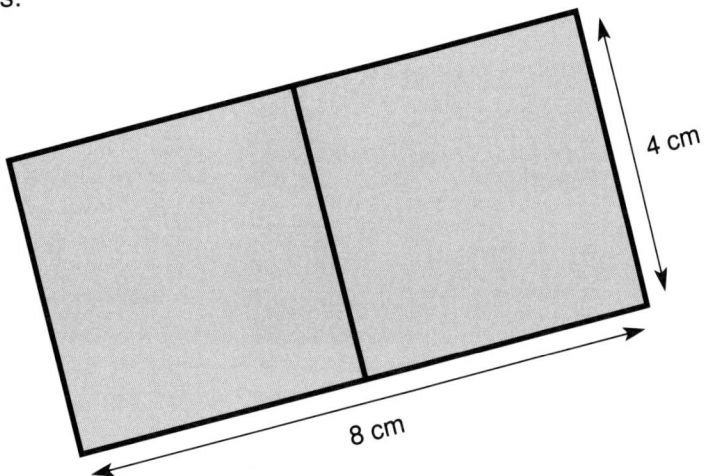

4 cm
8 cm

Use your dominoes to make this chain.

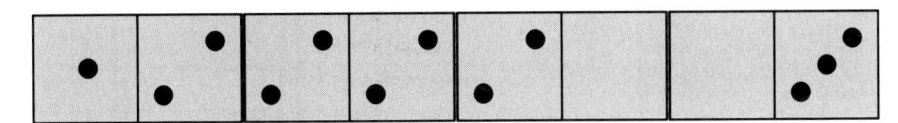

Add more of the dominoes to the chain.
Make the chain as long as you can.

11 How many of your dominoes have you used?

12 Can you make a matching chain which uses the whole DOUBLE 3 set?

Make the 5 extra dominoes for a DOUBLE 4 set.

13 Can you use the whole DOUBLE 4 set to make one matching chain?

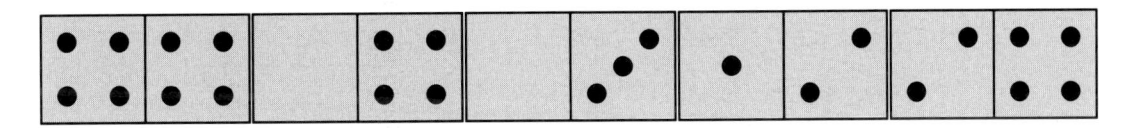

Use your dominoes to make this chain.

14 What rule has been used to decide how to join the dominoes together?

15 Make the longest chain you can using this rule. How many dominoes have you used?

16 Think of a rule of your own. What is the longest chain you can make using your rule?

The Nielson Line

The Nielson Line owns 4 cargo ships.

The cargo is packed in crates like this.

Each crate measures 1 m × 1 m × 1 m.
Its volume is 1 cubic metre (1 m^3).
It holds 1 m^3 of cargo.

1. What volume of cargo will:
   a. 2 crates hold?
   b. 6 crates hold?
   c. 10 crates hold?

2. How many crates are there:
   a. in stack X?
   b. in stack Y?

3. What is the volume of cargo:
   a. in stack X?
   b. in stack Y?

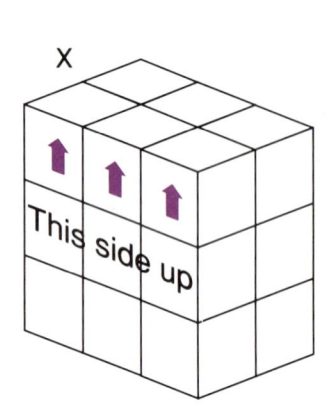

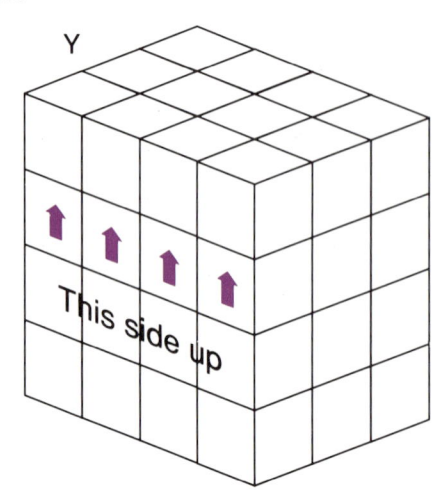

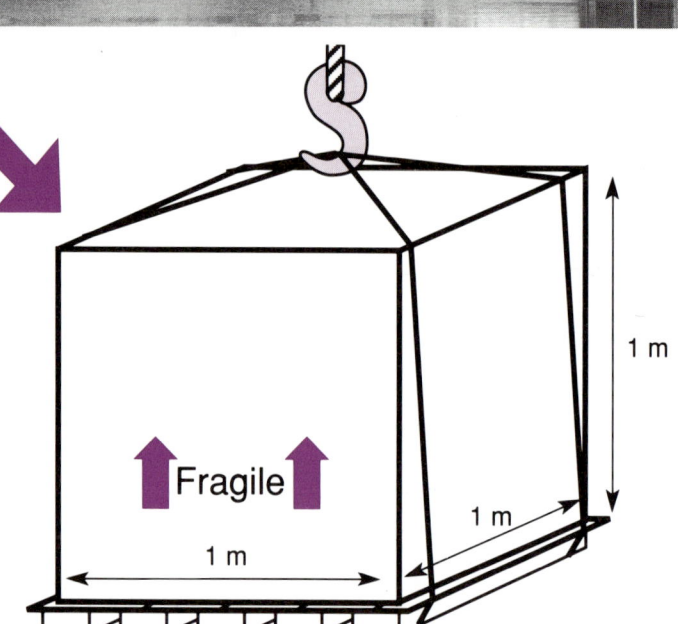

The Nielson Line

The *Sea Dove* is one of the ships in the Nielson Line.

This is the view of the *Sea Dove* from above.

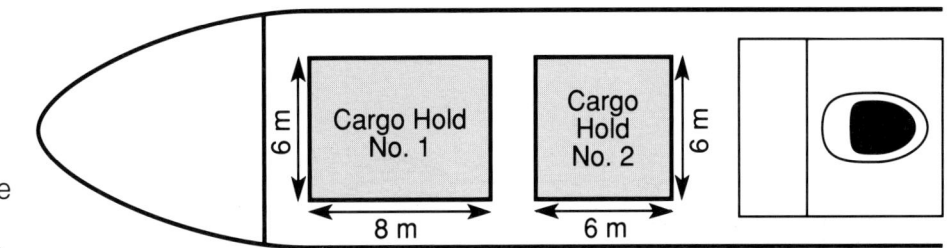

4 How many crates can be fitted on the floor:
   a of Cargo Hold No. 1?
   b of Cargo Hold No. 2?

This is a side view of the *Sea Dove*.

5 How many layers of crates can be fitted:
   a into Cargo Hold No. 1?
   b into Cargo Hold No. 2?

6 How many crates altogether can be packed:
   a into Cargo Hold No. 1?
   b into Cargo Hold No. 2?

7 What volume of cargo can be packed:
   a into Cargo Hold No. 1?
   b into Cargo Hold No. 2?
   c into the *Sea Dove*?

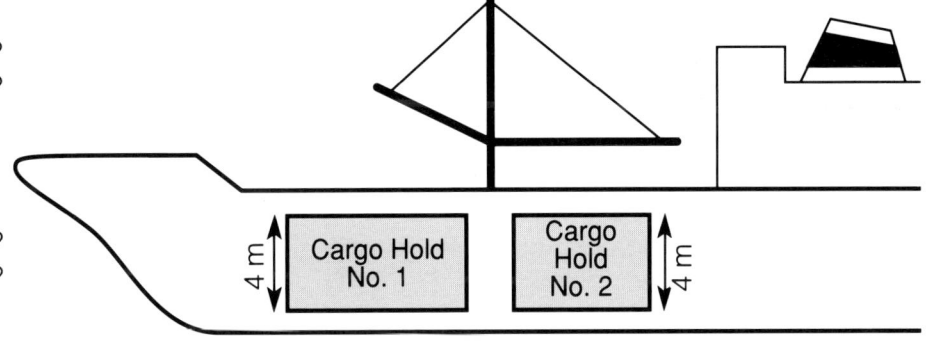

A customer wants the Nielson Line to transport 695 crates of cargo from London to Amsterdam.

8 Copy this table. Fill it in.

Nielson Line ship	Hold No.1 measurements	Volume of cargo when full (m³)	Hold No.2 measurements	Volume of cargo when full (m³)	Total cargo for both holds (m³)
Sea Dove	8m × 6m × 4m	192	6m × 6m × 4m	144	336
North Star	9m × 5m × 4m		6m × 5m × 4m		
The Oslo	8m × 6m × 4m		7m × 5m × 4m		
Nielson	9m × 6m × 4m		6m × 6m × 4m		

9 Two ships will have to be used to transport the cargo. Which two are they?

Decision Trees

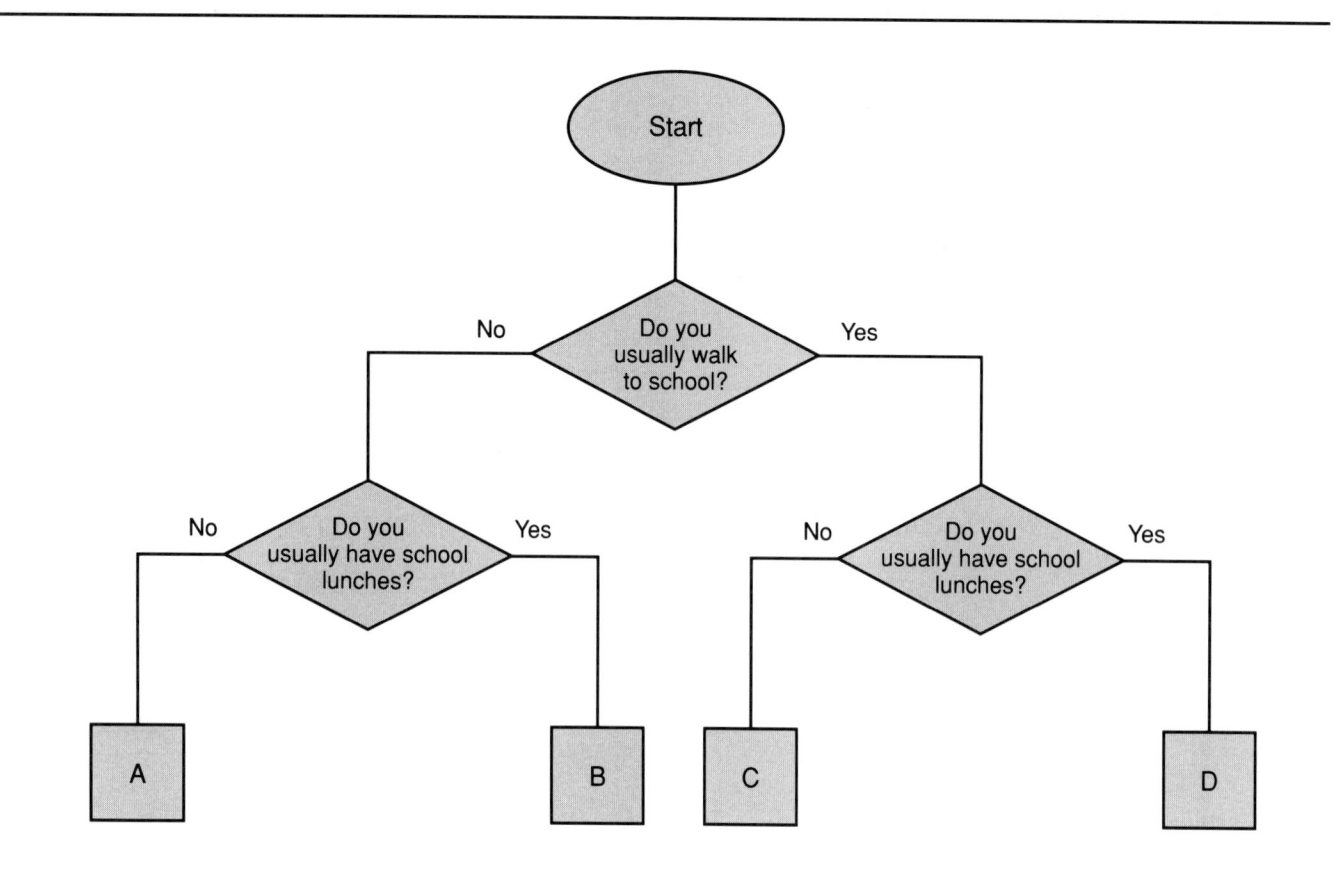

```
                    Start
                      |
              Do you usually
         No ← walk to school? → Yes
         ↓                        ↓
   Do you usually          Do you usually
No ← have school → Yes   No ← have school → Yes
    lunches?                 lunches?
   ↓         ↓              ↓           ↓
   A         B              C           D
```

1. Follow through the diagram. Answer the questions.
   Find which category you belong to: A, B, C or D.

2. Jason Jones belongs to category A. Marion Marlow belongs to category B.
   Alan Smith belongs to category C. Debbie Reed belongs to category D.
   a Who walks to school and has school lunches?
   b Who does not walk to school and does not have school lunches?
   c Who walks to school but does not have school lunches?
   d Who does not walk to school but has school lunches?

3. Find a person in your class who belongs to:
   a Category A,
   b Category B,
   c Category C,
   d Category D.

4. We can write any results from the decision tree in a table like this:
   Copy the table.

	Usually has school lunch	Does not have school lunches
Usually walks to school		
Does not walk to school		

Write the names of the people you found in question **3** in the table.

Decision Trees

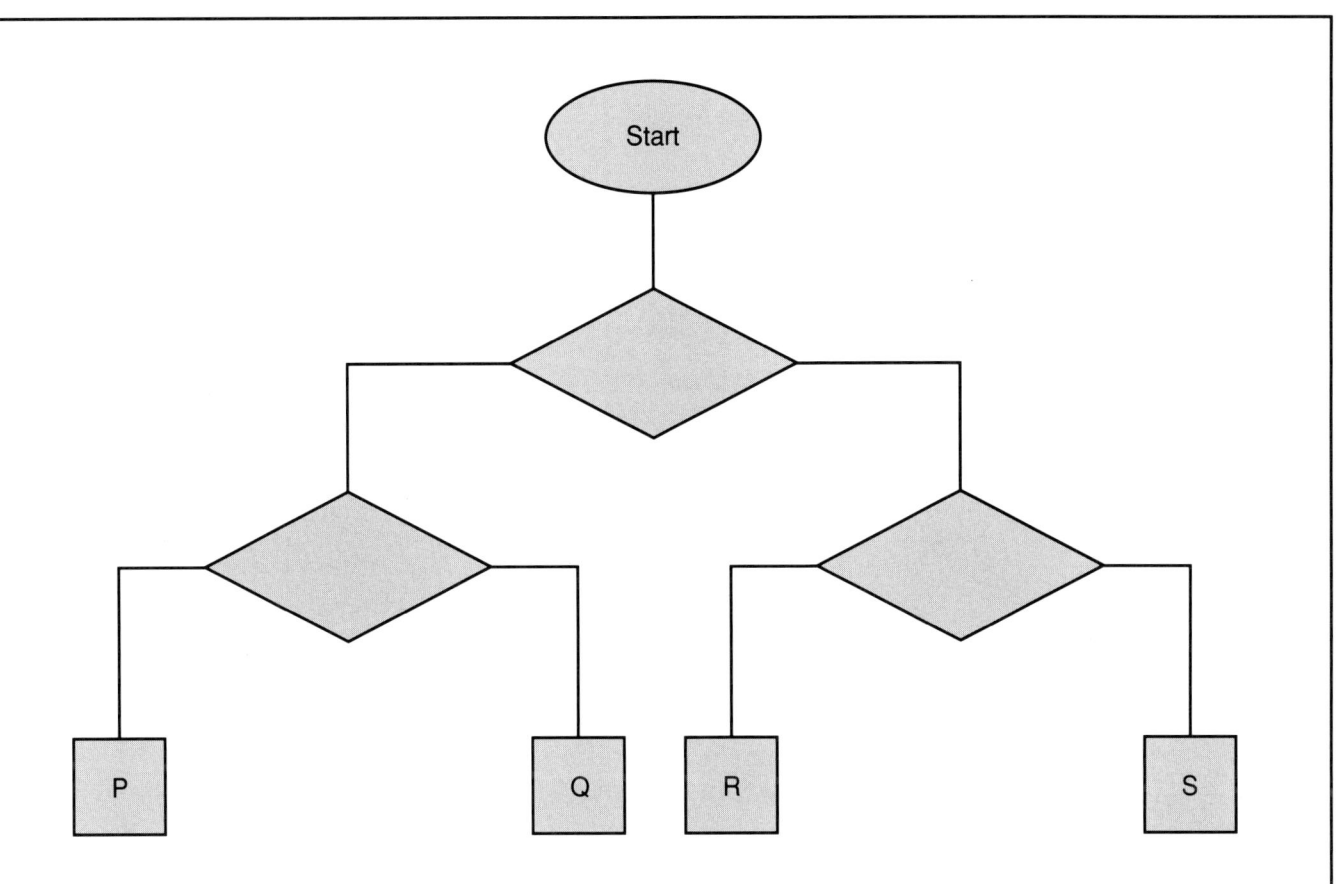

5 Copy the diagram onto a blank page.
Write questions in each ◇ so that your diagram divides people into:
Category P: likes maths but does not like PE
Category Q: likes maths and PE
Category R: does not like maths or PE
Category S: does not like maths but likes PE.

6 Find a person in your class who belongs to:
  a Category P,   b Category Q,   c Category R,   d Category S.

7 Draw a decision tree diagram which goes with this table:

	Has at least one brother	Has no brother
Has at least one sister		
Has no sisters		

Name the categories in your decision tree W, X, Y, Z.

8 Find a person in your class who belongs to each category W, X, Y, Z.

Designing a House

Gerry and Maggie are getting married.

This is the architect's scale drawing of their new house.

1. Measure the height of the door on the drawing.

2. The scale the architect used is one of A – D:
   a. It is not 1 cm to 200 cm.
      Explain how you can tell.
   b. Which scale do you think is correct?

A 1 cm to 200 cm

B 1 cm to 150 cm

C 1 cm to 100 cm

D 1 cm to 50 cm

3. The bedroom window is $3\frac{1}{2}$ metres wide. How tall is it?

4. What are the dimensions, in metres, of the large downstairs window?

5. How tall is the house at its tallest point?

6. How many metres wide is it, including the flat-roofed section?

Draw a house.

7. You need centimetre squared paper.
   Use a scale of 1 : 50.

   Make your own architect's drawing of the house.

   1 cm to 50 cm

Designing a House

This is the architect's plan
of the building site.

8 On the plan, what is the width of
   the house including the flat-roofed section?

9 The scale on the plan is one of A – D:

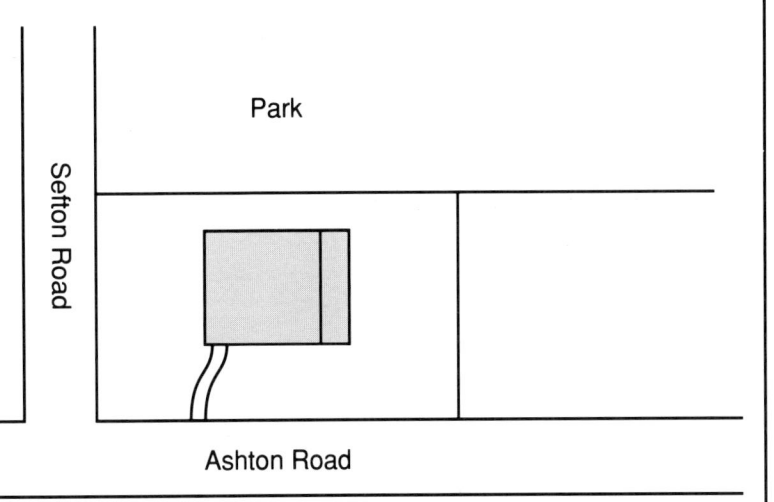

   A 1 cm to 1 m
   B 1 cm to 3 m
   C 1 cm to 5 m
   D 1 cm to 10 m

   Which one is it?
   Explain how you know.

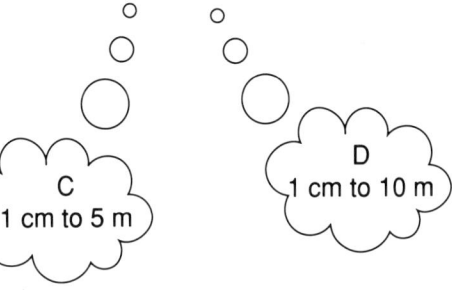

10 The garden fence along
   Ashton Road is 25 metres long.
   How long is the fence along Sefton Road?

This is a plan of the ground floor of the house.
The scale is 1 centimetre to 2 metres.

11 Write down the dimensions of each room in metres.

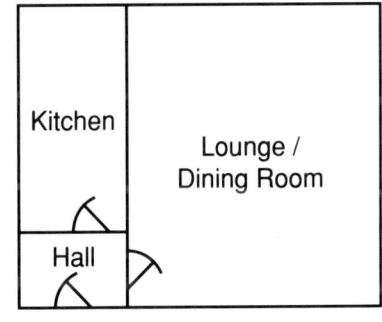

DESIGN YOUR OWN HOUSE

12 Use 1 cm squared paper. Think about the house that you would
   like to live in. Imagine that you are the architect.
   Draw a front view of your dream house.
   Use a scale of 1 : 100.

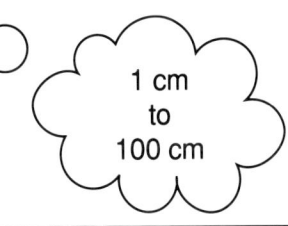

   1 cm to 100 cm

Oil at Sea

NEWS FLASH *** MONDAY 10 TH JULY

GREEK TANKER SANTOS HOLED OFF NEWPORT...

9.00 A.M. TODAY...

20 000 TONNES OIL ON BOARD. POLLUTION THREAT...

TANKER HERON RUSHING TO SCENE WITH PUMPING EQUIPMENT.

1 When was the *Santos* holed? Give the day, date and time.

2 How many tonnes of oil was she carrying?

This graph shows how much oil spilled into the sea between 9.00 a.m. and 3.00 p.m. on Monday.

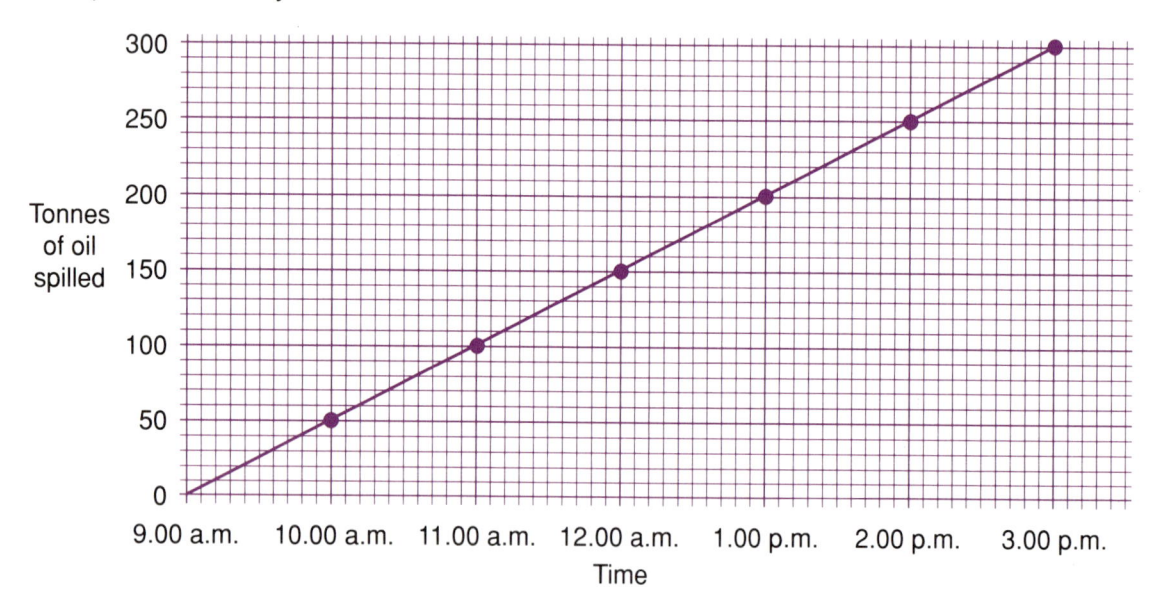

3 How many tonnes of oil had spilled into the sea:
 a by 10.00 a.m.?
 b by 11.00 a.m.?
 c by 12 a.m.?
 d by 1.00 p.m.?

4 How many tonnes of oil spilled into the sea each hour?

5 If the *Santos* continued to lose oil at the same rate, how much oil would have been spilled into the sea:
 a by 5.00 p.m. Monday?
 b by 9.00 p.m. Monday?
 c by 9.00 a.m. Tuesday?

Oil at Sea

NEWS FLASH * TUESDAY 11 TH JULY**

PUMPING OPERATIONS ON SANTOS BEGAN AT 9.00 A.M. TUESDAY...

NO MORE OIL BEING SPILLED INTO SEA.

300 TONNES OIL PER HOUR BEING PUMPED OFF SANTOS ONTO HERON.

6   When did the *Santos* stop spilling oil into the sea? Give the day, date and time.

7   How long was this after she was first holed?

8   How much oil had spilled into the sea by this time?

9   How much oil was left to be pumped off by the *Heron*?

10 How many tonnes of oil did *Heron* pump off:
    a   each hour?
    b   in 12 hours?
    c   each day?

11 How much oil was left in the *Santos* after one day's pumping?

12 Copy this graph.

    Finish it to show how much oil was left in the *Santos* at 9.00 a.m. each day.

13 a   On what day was the *Santos* emptied of oil?
    b   About what time did pumping operations end?

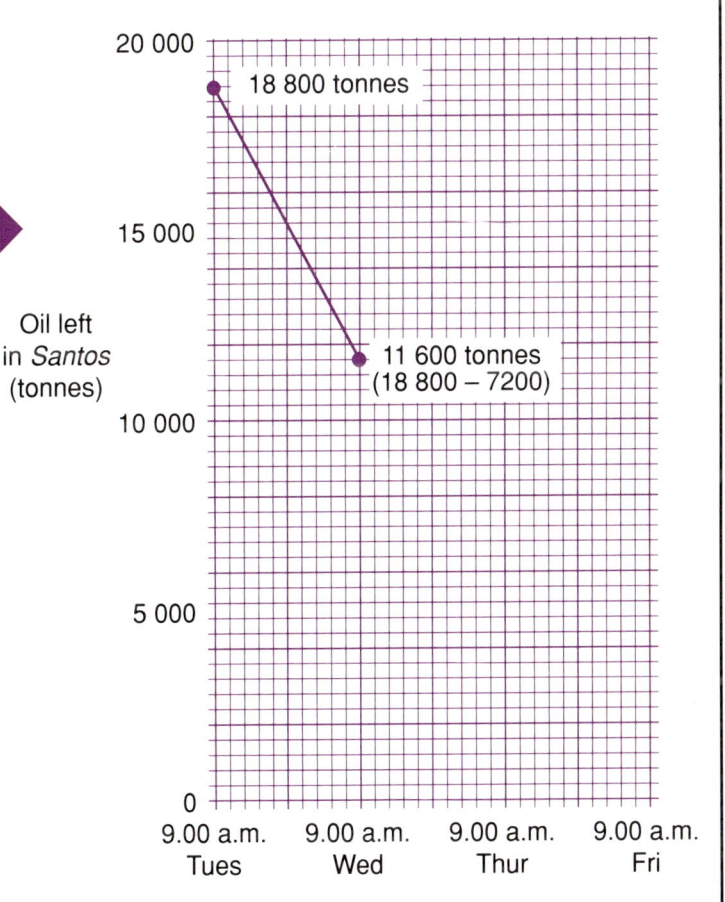

Instant Credit

Price's Bikes

100 cc cylinder engine
Maximum speed 120 km/h
Tank capacity 7.8 litres

★ Cash price £800
★ or use Price's low cost credit scheme
★ Deposit 30%
★ Balance paid over 12 months
★ Interest rate 20%

Gill wants a bike like Dave's – the Suzuki 100 in the advert.

1 What is the bike's maximum speed?
2 How much petrol does the tank hold?
3 Dave paid cash for his bike. How much did he pay?

Gill decides to buy her bike using Price's Credit Scheme.

4 What percentage of the cash price will she have to pay as a deposit?
5 Over how many months can the balance be paid?
6 What rate of interest will she have to pay on this balance?

Instant Credit

Gill works out how much the bike will cost.
She uses the credit card to help her.

7 Copy the card. Fill in the cash price.

Gill has to pay a 30% cash deposit.

8 What is:
   a 10% of £800?
   b 30% of £800?

9 What cash deposit will Gill have to pay?
   Fill this in on your credit card.

10 What balance will be left to pay off?
    Fill in the balance on your card.

Gill will be charged 20% interest on the balance.

11 What is:
    a 10% of £560?
    b 20% of £560?

12 Fill in on your credit card the interest Gill will have to pay.

13 Add together the balance and the interest. Fill this in on your card.

14 Gill has 12 months to pay. Fill in her monthly repayments on your card.

15 How much will Gill pay for her bike altogether?

16 How much more than Dave will she pay for her bike?

Credit Card Gill Greenaway	£
Cash Price	800
Deposit (30%)	
Balance	
Interest on balance (20%)	
Total Repayments (Balance + interest)	
Monthly repayment	

IN YOUR CAR

Look at the advertisement for cars.

Choose the one you would like to own.

17 Write down its cash price.

18 Work out how much you would pay using Price's Credit scheme.

19 How much would you save by paying cash?

YES! WE'VE DONE IT AGAIN   *This Week Only!*

AUDI Coupé injection, 2.2, blue	£4995
AUDI 100 GL 5E, 4d, 2.1, blue	£2995
AUSTIN Metro L, 5d, 1.3, silver	£5695
AUSTIN Rover 216 S, 4d, 1.6, white	£6495
AUSTIN Montego L, 4d, 1.6, beige	£4995
AUSTIN Montego HL, 4d, 1.6, blue	£4795
AUSTIN Maestro, 5d, 1.0, white	£3595
AUSTIN Metro, white	£2995
AUSTIN Metro MG, 3d, 1.3, red	£3795
AUSTIN Maestro HLS, 5d, 1.6, gold	£3395
AUSTIN Rover 2300 S Auto, 5d, 2.3, blue	£2995
AUSTIN Maestro, 5d, 1.3, white	£3795
AUSTIN Rover 2300, 2.3, green	£3195
AUSTIN Metro S, 3d, 1.3, bronze	£2795
BMW 316, 4d, 1.8, red	£6995
CITROEN Visa Super X, 5d, 1.1, black	£2495
FSO Saloon, 4d, 1.5, red	£2995
FSO 125P Estate, 1.5, grey	£2995
FIAT 127, 2d, 1.0, yellow	£1895
FORD Escort L Auto, 5d, 1.6, blue	£7495

A Place to Live

Last year 100 teenage couples were married in Hilperton.

This pie chart tells you about their first homes.

1. a What percentage of the 100 couples bought their own home?
   b How many couples is this?

2. a What percentage of the couples did not buy their own home?
   b How many couples is this?

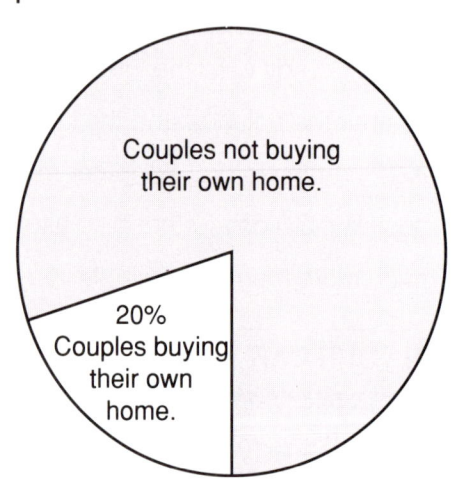

Couples not buying their own home.

20% Couples buying their own home.

This pie chart is about the 80 couples who did not buy their own home.

3. You can see that half of them lived in rented accommodation.
   a What percentage is this?
   b How many couples is this?

4. a What percentage of the 80 couples lived with their parents?
   b How many couples is this?

5. a What percentage of the couples lived in a council flat?
   b How many couples is this?

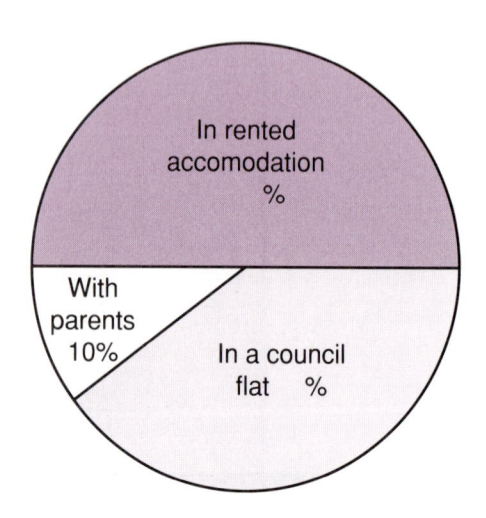

In rented accomodation %

With parents 10%

In a council flat %

A Place to Live

When Karen and Geoff Hart were first married they lived with Karen's parents.

They were put on the Council Housing List on January 1st.

6 a How many couples were on the list?
  b What position were the Harts?

7 15% of the 200 couples were housed in January. How many couples is this?

8 At the end of January:
  a who was top of the list?
  b what position were the Harts?

9 20% of the 170 couples left on the list were housed in February. How many couples is this?

10 What position were the Harts at the end of February?

11 50% of the 136 couples left on the list were housed in March. How many couples were left on the list at the end of March?

Tintown Council Housing List
January 1st

1	Butcher	L & D
2	Grisman	P & T
3	Laine	E & R
4	Roberts	S & J
5	Sighan	F & S

30	Chan	R & I
31	Davids	A & K
32	Smith	F & A
33	James	R & J
34	Francis	J & P
35	Ahmed	F & Z

195	Turner	A & V
196	Lee	H & M
197	Edwards	R & L
198	Brown	C & S
199	Curtis	R & N
200	Hart	L & G

The council housed 9 couples every month for the rest of the year.

12 What position were the Harts at the end of April?

13 Copy this table. Fill it in.

Month ending	31st Jan	25th Feb	31st Mar	30th Apr	31st May	30th June	31st July	31st Aug	30th Sept
The Hart's position on the list	170	136	68						

14 In which month were Karen and Geoff housed?

Finding a name

Jim and Carol have been married for two years. They have just had their first child – a boy. But they can't decide which of these names to choose.

| Ben | Harry | Grant |

They decide to put the three names in a hat and choose one.

1. How many different possible names can be chosen from the hat?

2. How many cards in the hat have Ben written on them?

3. The chance that Ben will be chosen as the baby's name is **one out of three**, or $\frac{1}{3}$ (because there are three cards and one has Ben on it).
   What is the chance that Grant will be chosen as the baby's name? Why?

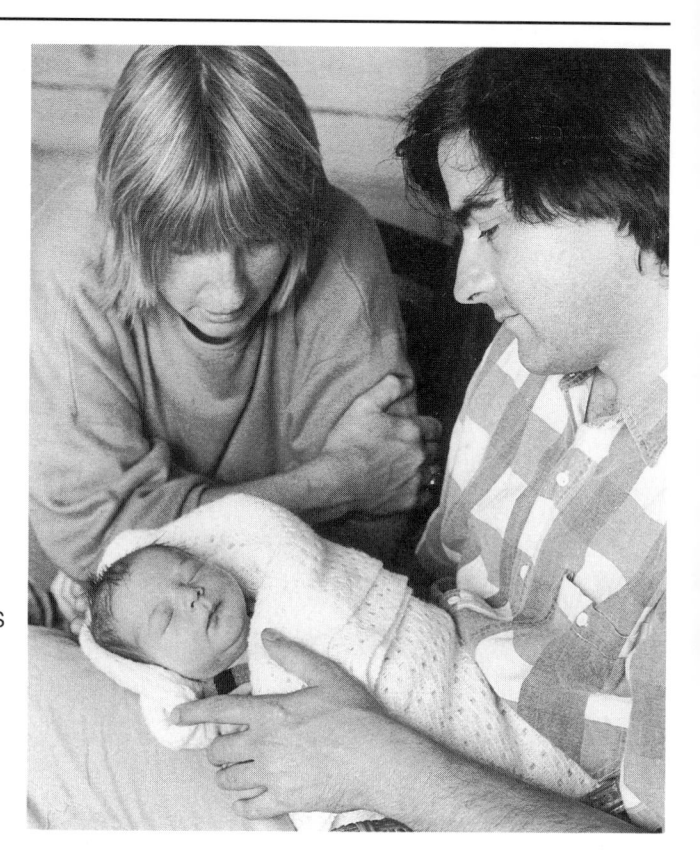

Winston and Pattie have also just had their first baby – a girl.

They too can't decide on a name.
The grandparents want various names.
Winston and Pattie have their own ideas.
Eventually they decide to put all six ideas in a hat and draw out the name:

| Sally | Sarah | Betty |
| Grandma 1 | Grandma 2 | Grandad 1 |

| Alice | Sarah | Betty |
| Grandad 2 | Winston | Pattie |

4. The chance that 'Sarah' will be chosen is **two out of six** or $\frac{2}{6}$ because there are six cards and two of them have 'Sarah' written on them.
   What is the chance that 'Betty' will be chosen? Why?

5. What is the chance that 'Alice' will be chosen?

6. What is the chance that the name that Grandma 2 wants will be chosen?

Finding a name

This spinner is for people who can't decide what name to choose for their cat or dog.

You write names in the sections and spin the choice.

7 Using this spinner what is the chance that your cat would be called 'Scruff'? Why?

8 Using this spinner explain why the chance that your dog will be called 'Henry' is $\frac{3}{8}$.

9 What is the chance that your dog will be called:
   a Fido?
   b Blip?

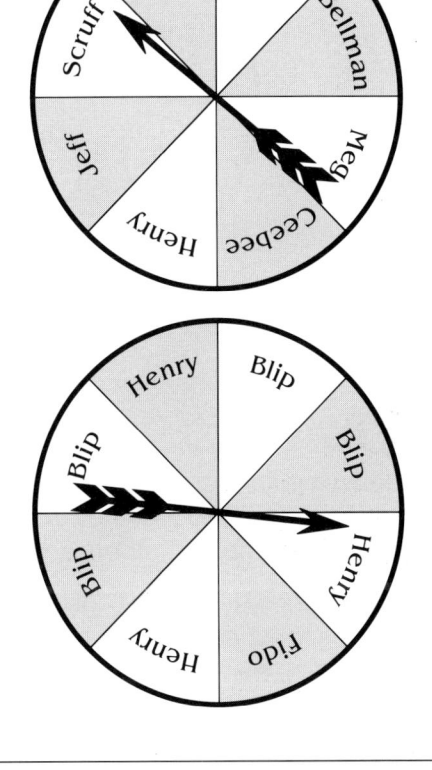

IN A SPIN

Pedigree dogs have long 'kennel names'
For example:

   'Bad Bellman of Boa'
   or 'Barnaby Golden Gunner'.

You can make up your own kennel names using the spinners.
For example, you can make:

   'Maytime Field Grey'
   or 'Maytime Gold Edge', etc.

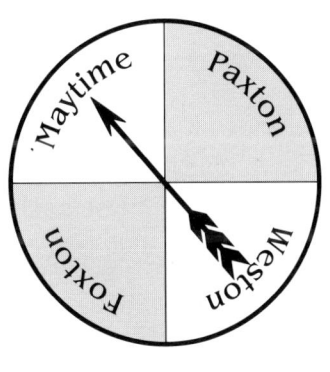

First Part of Kennel Name

Second Part of Kennel Name

10 a How many different names can be made? List them.
   b What is the chance that, after spinning both spinners, the name you make is 'Paxton High Noon'?

Working with eight

Here are the numbers from 1 to 8. Each group of 4 has the same total.

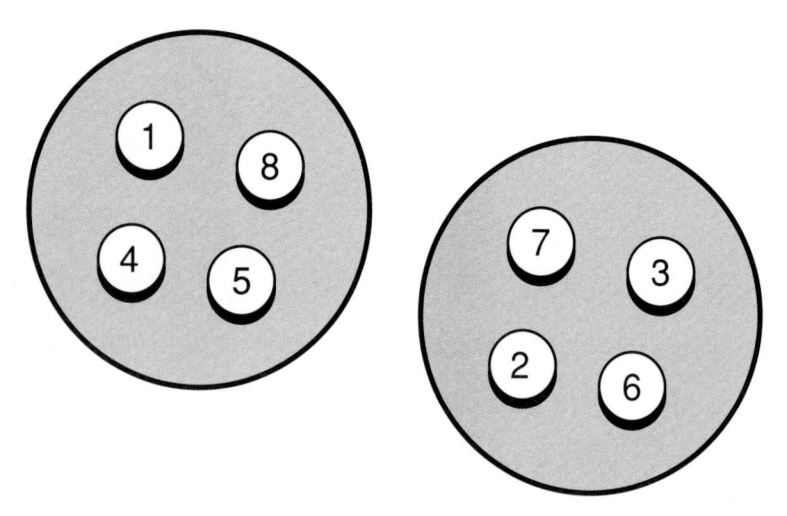

1 What does each group of four add up to?

2 a Write down a different way of grouping four of the numbers from 1 to 8 so that they add up to 18.
   b What do the other four numbers add up to?

3 Arrange the numbers from 1 to 8 into two different groups of four so that each group has the same total. How many ways of doing this can you find? List them all.

4 Four of the numbers from 1 to 8 have been used in this addition. Replace the ? by the other four numbers so that the answer is less than 10 000.

$$+\begin{array}{cccc} 5 & 1 & 3 & 7 \\ ? & ? & ? & ? \end{array}$$

5 Arrange the numbers from 1 to 8 in this addition to give an answer:
   a as large as possible,
   b as small as possible.

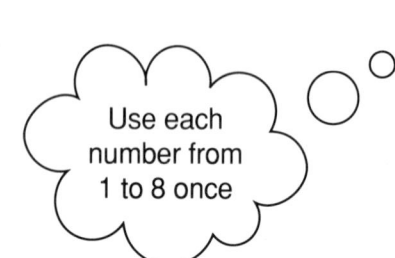

Use each number from 1 to 8 once

$$+\begin{array}{cccc} ? & ? & ? & ? \\ ? & ? & ? & ? \end{array}$$

MAKE A HUNDRED

6 a Arrange the numbers from 1 to 8 in a calculation which has an answer of exactly 100. You may use each number more than once.
   b How many ways can you find of doing this?

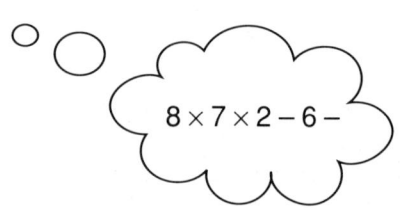

$8 \times 7 \times 2 - 6 -$